Skyrocket Your Sales and Profits!

How to Know Your Customers Better Than They Know Themselves

Marie J. Kane

Skyrocket Your Sales and Profits!
How to Know Your Customers Better Than They Know Themselves

ISBN 978-0-9762579-7-4
Library of Congress Control Number: 2010925166

Book Design by Ward Flynn
Cover Design by Cyanotype

Transformation PRESS

For Permissions requests, contact the author
240 Huntcliff Ct.
Fayetteville, GA 30214
770-461-3820
Marie@MarketRelationshipMastery.com

Printed in the United States of America, Charleston, S.C.

I dedicate this book to all the owners, executives and managers of small and medium size businesses worldwide. You create the jobs, provide the products and services, and make the economic contributions that make a difference in the lives of your employees, customers, communities and countries every day.

Acknowledgements

I would like to acknowledge my corporate consulting clients, who for over two and a half decades have honored me with their business and their trust. I would not have this knowledge to share today if it were not for my experience with these exceptional, forward-looking businesses and organizations.

I am indebted to Ken Bausch, Randy Baustert, Bonnie Bobbitt, Darbie Bufford, Elsom Eldridge, Ward Flynn, Carter Harkins, Cathy Kane, Candy Kaspers, Lynne Klippel, Alberta Lloyd, Jim Loesch, Bud Mingledorff, Peter Nicholas, Laura Pettyjohn, Judy Suiter and Melissa Wolfley for their generous input and support for this book.

My heartfelt thanks to all of you,
Marie

Table of Contents

Introduction

More than 25 years as a strategic business consultant has amply demonstrated to me the critical importance of an intimate and comprehensive understanding of your target market. This book was written to help your company more precisely meet the core needs and wants of your target market, so that you will maximize your sales, profits and long-term competitive advantage.

This book will show you how you can tap the enormous potential in strategically utilizing a market survey system to gather high-impact market intelligence, while you simultaneously strengthen your company's relationship with your target market and current customers.

Together, we will explore why and how you implement a strategic market survey system in your business.

Here is what you can expect to discover in this book:

- How to leverage an intimate knowledge of your market to optimize the impact on your sales

- An understanding of what a comprehensive, strategic market survey process is

- The surprising ways that your business will benefit from implementing strategic market surveys

- The importance of fully integrating your market intelligence gathering and customer relationship building practices with your strategic direction

- How to use surveys to create relationships with your current and prospective customers so that they cannot wait to spend their money with you

- How you can use surveys effectively with your current customers

- High-impact ways to use surveys in evaluating the potential of new products or services you are considering

- Ways to use market survey strategies to create greater competitive advantage

- What not to do when you implement this market survey strategy

- How to get the most out of using this market survey strategy

If you already do market surveys or have familiarity with survey processes and tools, in this book you will find new ideas on more effective or creative ways to use surveys to get better business results. Even if you are an old hand at market surveys, there are some surprises waiting for you within these pages.

If you are not currently a user of market surveys, no problem! There are plenty of "mini-processes" and lists offered throughout the book. These will show you what to do to get started.

Regardless of your experience level, you will find something of value here. You can create much more positive impact for your business with this strategy than most companies ever imagine. Whatever your use of market surveys has been in the past, what you will uncover in these pages will help you take your company to the next level.

In the **Afterword,** I have some very **special gifts** to help you get started. I invite and encourage you to make use of them to propel your business to greater heights. Join me to discover how a strategic market survey approach will grow your company's sales, profits and competitive advantage!

Marie Kane
March 2010

Chapter One

Skyrocket Your
Sales and Profits

*"How much money is your company
leaving on the table?"*

Chapter One
Skyrocket Your Sales and Profits

What is the key to vastly improving your company's sales and profits? How do you get customers to do business with your company, instead of your competition? The answer lies in how current and prospective customers make buying decisions.

Whom do we do business with? We do business with companies and with people whom we know, like and trust. We do business with companies that provide the product or service that best meets our specific wants and needs. We do business with the company that solves our problems, fulfills our desires and gives us the best value for our dollar.

Summary of Factors in Customer Buying Decisions

➢ Relationship

- Know you, like you, trust you

- Customer's best interests

➢ Emotional Fulfillment

- Meet needs and wants

- Fulfill core desires

- Lay fears to rest

➢ Concrete Benefit

- Good value for the dollar

- Solve a specific problem

- Support an opportunity

When customers see that you have their best interests at heart and that you will provide the best solution to their problem or fulfill their deepest desire, it is a very strong inducement to do business with you. Whether your customer is an end user consumer or another business, a human being makes the buying decision.

Intimate Customer Knowledge and Relationships Are the Key

You must know exactly what your customers want, do not want, and fear. You must have insight into what is in the heads and hearts of your current customers and prospects. When you do, and you apply that intimate knowledge and understanding of your customers, you create sustainable competitive advantage.

The secret is to build quality relationships, not just make transactions.

Are your customers raving fans who will not take their business elsewhere, even when it might be cheaper, even when they have concern about money?

Business *is* people. People make decisions emotionally to a significant degree and then justify them rationally. Relationships are the key. Exploration and engagement with your current and prospective customers is what successful business is all about. You cannot connect powerfully with your customers if you do not have a specific understanding of exactly how you will make their life or business better in relation to the service or product you offer.

What your customers want is very often different from what you think they need. Even more challenging is that what they tell you they want is not always their deepest want, the one you really have to satisfy to "hit a home run" with them. This is not because they want to lie to you, it is because they are sometimes not fully conscious themselves of what they want or need. They do know what they feel about the impact of your product or service on their life or business.

How much are assumptions about your target market or current customers costing your company?

Let me tell you some stories. You can learn something from each one about what can help or hurt your company on the road to success. There are multiple scenarios to help you explore the different factors that can impact your sales. I encourage you to stop and think about the questions posed after each story so that you get the most out of each example.

Company A is doing pretty well. They have not had their best year ever, but their sales are moderately good and their profits are adequate. Things have been challenging for them, and they are pleased to be doing better than other companies in their industry are. They do have questions about the future. Their industry is undergoing change, and their target market's expectations have changed even more. They want to be sure that they are positioned for future success. They do not want to be lulled into a false sense of security, just because they are stable at the present.

What concerns do you have about the future of your company?

Company B is in a very different situation. Their sales are falling. Their employee morale is down, and their best people are leaving the company. Their profits are rapidly shrinking. Unless they turn things around very soon, they are going to be out of business. Their competition seems always to have the edge.

What is the source of your company's competitive advantage?

Are you building on that optimally?

If not, what is the first step you could take in that direction?

What is it that your customers really value that you do better, or could do better, than your competition?

Is there an opportunity to build further on that to increase your competitive edge?

Do you know enough about your target market to take these steps confidently?

Look at another scenario. Company C has launched a new product that they put a great deal of money into developing and marketing. Customers are indifferent and sales are well below expectations. The negative impact on the bottom line of the company is substantial. The news in the business press is affecting their credibility in the industry. This has caused customers to shy away and their sales to fall even further. They believe that they can recover from this mistake, but it is going to take a lot of time and effort.

How do you approach developing a new product or service?

Do you know with certainty exactly what your market wants and needs?

Do you create interest and excitement in your market in advance of your new product or service launch?

Now we look at another business situation. Company D is an acknowledged leader in their industry. They stay extremely close to their current customers and are always reaching out to their target market, so that they can spot the coming trends. Their sales are strong, even in challenging times, and their bottom line is very healthy.

What strategic initiatives are you considering to maintain or create a similar position for your company?

Check out a situation that is not so happy. Company E launched a new product successfully and thought they had it made. Initial sales exceeded their wildest expectations. Unfortunately, within six months of the product launch, customer service crashed because they were not prepared for what their customers expected. The more the complaint rate soared, the more their reputation sank. This situation sucked attention away from other parts of their business, which then began to suffer as well. As consumer confidence eroded, so did their bottom line. If they did not stop the freefall soon, the company could be in serious trouble.

What steps do you have in place to assess your customers' expectations on a regular basis?

How often do you evaluate your customer support strategy and practices to ensure that they keep pace with your customer demands and shifting market expectations?

Which of These Apply to Your Business?

- Our sales are down from what they once were

- We are doing fairly well, but would like to do better in sales and profits

- We want more market share than we have now

- We need stronger competitive advantage to secure our future

- We have cash flow problems

- Our profit margin is not where we want it to be

- We would like to be more confident that our products and services are what the market really wants

How Many of These Pertain to Your Business?

- We need a better understanding of our customers' problems and what will make them buy from us, instead of someone else

- We need to ensure that what we are offering is what our market is most willing to buy

- We want a way to reach out to our prospects that will not be too costly

- We have a good competitive edge in our market and want to ensure that we keep it

- We are concerned that our customers may shop for the cheapest solution rather than staying loyal to us

- Our customer retention rate is slipping, and we have got to do something about it

- We want to be sure our sales and customer service people represent us in the best way possible

Do You See Your Company Here?

- We want more referral business from our current customers than we are getting now

- We need to make certain that the market is enthusiastic about our new products or services

- We focus on leveraging our marketing dollars to the max

- We need to cement a stronger relationship with our current customers

- We are always on the lookout for effective ways to keep our sales force sharp

- We want to ensure that we supply the value that our customers expect

- We need to regain some momentum that we have lost

- We are doing well, and we want to ensure that it continues that way and gets even better

There is one strategy that will help in every situation listed above. That strategy is for a company to gather and effectively apply high-impact market intelligence, while they simultaneously create or build stronger relationships with their current and prospective customers.

The Impact of Knowing Your Customer Inside and Out

Company F aspired to be the leader in their market, but they were struggling with customer retention. They decided that the solution was to launch a new product, one that they had been seriously considering for some time. They decided to get input first from their target market and current customers on what they were so seriously considering. They understood that they had to be right about the need that they were trying to meet for their customers, both current and prospective.

As a result, they discovered that the product that they thought they should create, one that was going to require a substantial amount of time and money, was not the product that their customers wanted. They not only avoided wasting all that time and money, but in the process, they also discovered exactly what their customers did want. This put them in a very advantageous position to move forward.

What did they do then? They built and launched the desired product, and their sales increased significantly. They followed up with their customers and prospects on a regular basis, gathering even more precise market intelligence on exactly how to improve their product and service. They entered into an ongoing dialogue with their customers.

Based on the customer feedback, they improved their product and service. Their sales rose yet again. Because of their ongoing dialogue with their customers and the marketplace, they discovered that there was a demand for an entire new suite of products that was a perfect fit with their company's expertise and strategic direction.

They implemented a two-year development process to bring out three new products. During that time, they stayed in close contact with their current and prospective customers. Through that process, they developed a list of people eagerly awaiting the new product releases.

This is pure gold - people lining up to eagerly hand you their money.

They successfully launched all three of those products because they knew exactly what their customers wanted and how they wanted it delivered and supported. Their new products and their customer service got rave reviews. The company's sales and profitability soared.

These kinds of results occur when companies consistently build intimate, transparent, ongoing relationships with their market and current customers. Imagine understanding your customers' wants, desires and fears so well that you can take highly focused, extremely profitable action every time!

What Is Your Company's Story?

Maybe things are not going well and you need a strategy to get out of the hole you are in. On the other hand, maybe your company is doing fairly well, but sales are growing very slowly, if at all.

Are your sales or profits below expectations?

Are expenses continuing to inch up day-by-day or, like kangaroos, in leaps and bounds?

Maybe nothing dramatic is happening, but the lack of progress means you are slowly sliding backwards, like sinking into slow-acting quicksand. In business, there is no such thing as standing still.

Maybe your company is doing pretty well. Sales and profits are climbing slowly, but steadily and your company is not in any danger, but you are convinced you can do a lot better.

What does it take to get a sharper competitive edge? When you know *how to enter the conversation already going on in your target customers' minds* that is when they will come running to do business with your company.

You know that a critical key to success in business is having an in-depth understanding of your customers' desires, needs, and fears and then providing the products and services that match them every single time. Applied knowledge is power! How do you gain this knowledge about your marketplace? It is simple. You ask them! Then you apply what you have learned strategically.

What If This Was Your Company's Story?

We have grown our sales and profits exponentially because:

- We know our customers' and our prospects' wants, needs, desires, and fears

- Our product development is tailored precisely to our market's issues

- We offer only products and services that our customers are willing to pay for now

- We get a great return on investment from laser-focused marketing campaigns

- We have built a strong foundation for the future

- We have enormous trust and credibility with our customer base

Keep going, the good news just keeps getting better.

- Our referral rate is constantly growing

- We have great repeat business

- Our customer retention rate is terrific

- It is easy to get continuous input from our customers because of our strong, ongoing relationship with them

- We have an incredibly motivated sales force

- We consistently beat our competition by a wide margin

There is still more.

- We are a leader in our industry and our market

- Stockholders, family members and employees are really happy

- High quality job applicants are beating down our door

- Customers passionately refer others

- Products and services are targeted to what our customers and prospects are looking for and willing to pay for

- We have created sustainable competitive advantage

How Do You Make This Your Company's Story?

You create the results listed above through the power of applied knowledge and relationships. Companies routinely leave money on the table by failing to take advantage of the opportunity to accomplish these two things simultaneously. You can gather and apply excellent market intelligence, while simultaneously building quality relationships.   This combination will drive significant increases in sales and profits and build a foundation for the future.

How do companies prosper in good times and challenging ones? They create unassailable competitive advantage.   Your products, services and customer service must make your target customers intent on buying from your company, instead of your competition. Review what it takes to accomplish this.

- Your product or service has to address their true wants and needs, as well as allay their fears

- You have to clearly be offering a solution to their problem, the answer to a deep desire or the key to a golden opportunity

- The value of your offering has to be clearly greater, from their point of view, than the price you are asking, so that you overcome any resistance they might have to buying

Once you have a strong relationship with your current customers and your prospective market, they trust that they can believe you. When you do come out with a product upgrade, new product or service, they are much more likely to believe your claims of what the product will do or how the service will meet a particular need.

This is most especially true if they know that they had a part in providing the input that shaped the product or service.   These customers and prospects constitute a ready-made market for that new product or service, if you keep the lines of communication open.

Determining Core Wants and Needs

If you only appeal to your customers' needs, however right you may be, they are much less likely to be attracted to your solution. If you only address their wants, but do not serve their needs, then your solution will only be a partial one that is not likely to be fully successful, and customer satisfaction will suffer as a result. The challenge for businesses is that what customers want and what they need do not always match, but you have to deliver on both.

Since customers are sometimes not conscious at the deepest level of their needs, wants and fears, your challenge is to dig them out. Many companies fail to uncover exactly what their customers want and what value they would place on it.   Many variables affect business success, like operational effectiveness and financial management, but no matter how well you do those things, if you do not offer what your customers want then you will not be successful.

Consider a real life example of deeply understanding the core need, want or problem that you are solving for your customer. Remember the old 33 RPM records? Well, some of us do. When it went the way of the dinosaur, the progression went from the 33 RPM record to the cassette tape, then to the CD and ultimately to the iPod.

What did customers say back then, when asked about the 33 RPM record? It costs too much and scratches too easily. The needles wear out the records and have to be replaced. We don't like the hissing noise in the background. There is no documentation of any record customer ever asking for the functions and advantages that came with the Compact Disk, let alone for something that cost MORE!

What if the music industry had been trapped by tunnel vision and had gone in the direction of creating better records that did not have the objectionable features brought up by customers, instead of uncovering what would best serve the customers' wants and needs, even the ones they were unaware of themselves. Where would we be then? Customers generally focus only on their current situation. You have to dig deep in interacting with your current customers and your target market, if you are to uncover their core desires, fears and needs.

Resist the temptation to decide what your customer needs based on inadequate information.   Resist the temptation to dive into product or service design before you have thoroughly explored the roots of what your customers really need and want from you. You will eventually get to the nuts and bolts of features, price, and so on. You do not want to start there. Start with exploring what is going on in your customers' heads and hearts. In relation to your company's products and services, you want to know what your customer would say in response to these questions:

What is the issue (problem or opportunity) that you are addressing?

What has been unsatisfactory when you have tried to address this issue in the past and why?

What is frustrating or frightening for you in dealing with this issue?

How would your life be better if this issue were successfully addressed?

In relation to this issue, what is happening that you do not want to have happen? What problem does that create in your life?

In relation to this issue, what is happening that is going the way you want it to? Why is that a good thing in relation to this issue?

These are just some examples of the kind of probing you need to do. You must start with no assumptions and then delve into what is going on with your customer or target market as deeply as you can, before drawing any conclusions. Assumptions cost you money, either wasted or left on the table, and seriously hinder your company's performance, competitive positioning, sales and profits.

If the situation for your target market is more an opportunity than a problem, you can explore similarly with questions focused on the nature of the opportunity, including not only what the customer expects to get out of that opportunity, but also why that outcome matters in the larger picture of their life or their business.

You can discover the problem your market is trying to solve. You can uncover what they desire. You can come to understand what they are afraid of and what they are trying to avoid. Then you are uniquely positioned to make product and service offerings that will speak directly to their core desires, and you will powerfully attract your market.

Customers, whether they are consumers or other businesses, are either running away from something or running toward something, sometimes both at the same time. If you understand what that is, then you are able to create and position your products and services accordingly. When you communicate effectively to your target market how what you have will solve their problem or allow them to grasp the desired opportunity, then your ability to create competitive advantage is significantly improved.

What One Strategy Addresses All These Scenarios?

About now, you may be thinking that all this makes sense, but how will you accomplish all this efficiently, economically and effectively? That is a good question. The answer is to apply a little known, little used strategy that employs market and customer surveys in a unique way.

The term "surveys" here does not mean the usual one-shot list of questions that is one-way communication with no follow-up sharing of results and decisions. We will be exploring a much richer scenario, one that will beautifully support the business success that you crave.

When you implement a process that allows you to gather market intelligence and simultaneously build and maintain a relationship with your market, then you increase your competitive advantage exponentially. Why? Remember, people buy from companies that they know, like and trust that provide top-notch solutions, which fulfill their wants, needs and desires, as well as allay their fears.

How Strategic Market Surveys Can Drive Up Your Sales

When you implement a strategic market and customer survey process, *you have a prime opportunity to address all three of the factors that drive your company's sales.* This is a major reason why you should not relegate doing market surveys simply to infrequent data gathering. When you merge in-depth market and customer intelligence gathering with relationship building, as part of a precisely orchestrated survey strategy to increase your sales, the return on investment (ROI) on implementing market surveys climbs astronomically. Consider how that works.

There are three ways to increase your sales:

1. Increase your prospect flow - get more people to encounter and consider your product or service.

2. Increase your sales conversion rate - increase the percentage of people who, upon being exposed to your product or service, proceed to buy it.

3. Increase your dollar value per customer - increase the amount that each customer spends with you.

How does implementing a strategic market survey system address these three factors? Consider increasing prospect flow. How do you get more people exposed to your product or service, regardless of your distribution channel? It might be a store, website, catalog or some other means of presenting and providing your product or service. One of the most common ways of attracting more prospects is marketing campaigns. What companies rarely consider is that you can use surveys to both gather and give information. You can do a little marketing while you are gathering information.

More importantly, once you have gathered and analyzed your information and you really understand your target market's inner fears and desires, then you can shape your marketing efforts precisely to what will attract them to consider your product or service. That includes using their own words describing their issue or problem. How would you get those words? By asking the right questions in narrative form and then mining the answers for the most evocative descriptions of their challenges and related desires.

Now, consider increasing your conversion rate. There is nothing more powerful as an inducement for potential customers to purchase your product or service than your company having the best possible solution to their problem or the product that fulfills their hearts' desire. The only way that you can create and offer that product or service is to know your current customers and market intimately. A well-executed strategic survey process gives you that.

Finally, consider increasing your dollar value per customer. Do you remember the story earlier about the company that did their market research so well? They stayed in touch with their customers throughout the process of developing and launching their product, as well as thereafter. You may recall that as a result they created several more products that they knew with certainty their customers wanted. They had a ready-made market when they launched those products. This gave them a double advantage. They had additional products to offer, and they had a hungry audience waiting for them. This is a prime scenario for increasing your dollar value per customer.

The participants who had been involved in the survey dialogue were already poised for the product launch. They knew it was coming because of their participation in the survey process. They had some emotional stake in the product because of they had given input and knew it was used. They were primed to buy at the point of the product launch. We will explore this in Chapter Five.

When you have the relationships and market intelligence that enable you to offer precisely targeted new products or services at regular intervals, it is a great way to increase your dollar value per customer. Your company will be able to make these superior offerings, because you succeeded in getting into the heads and hearts of your customers, current and prospective.

Another factor is the price of your products. Customers will often pay a premium when your product or service solves their problem or fulfills their desires significantly better than any other company's offerings.

When you increase any of these three leverage points that impact sales, it will improve your business results. Prospect flow, sales conversion and dollar value per customer are the lifeblood of sales performance.

The real payoff happens when you improve all three sales drivers simultaneously, because you get a synergistic, compounding effect that will exponentially improve your sales results. Companies have successfully doubled their sales and more in this manner.

Michael Gerber, the esteemed author of *The E-Myth Revisited* stated in that book that although the Marketing, Operations and Finance Departments each have their own accountabilities, "they share one common purpose - to make a promise their customer wants to hear, and to deliver on that promise better than anyone on the block!"

When you deeply understand your customers' wants, needs, fears and desires, then you know the promise to make. When you know how they want you to fulfill that promise that is when you can "deliver on that promise better than anyone on the block." When you do this consistently, you will continually drive greater sales, profits and competitive advantage for your business.

Companies leave money on the table when they do not know their customers and their market intimately. Many companies do not have this level of knowledge and understanding.

Is your company one of them?

When you get to know your customers and prospects, you also learn to "speak their language." In the course of interacting with them through your survey process, you learn how they think and speak about the issue that your product addresses. You can then offer products and services in a way that resonates with how they think and talk about their need or desire. One of the best ways to do that is to use their actual statements, which you would have obtained in the narrative questions in your surveys. People are more likely to buy when they recognize themselves in what you say.

When you can position yourself in this way, instead of trying to talk people into doing business with you, customers come to you. They experience that you are talking specifically to them and that you understand them. They find themselves thinking things like:

"That is really what I'm concerned about."

"That is exactly the problem I'm trying to solve!"

"That is just what I've imagined having!"

"I trust this company to stand behind their product."

"I believe they really care about their customers."

They make the purchase, not only because what you offer is exactly what they want and need, but also because they feel good about you as a company. Is your company positioned this way with your customers?

You may have done market research using surveys, or other techniques, for gathering information about the wants, needs, desires and fears of your target customers. BUT . . .

Did you build long lasting, loyal customer relationships as a result?

What happened after you got the information?

Did you analyze it, make a decision about what action to take and follow up?

Did you communicate your findings and plans back to your survey participants?

What was the impact on your bottom line?

Most businesses do not know how to create or capitalize on the competitive advantage that you can build with surveys. That power can be your company's when you use surveys for a dialogue with your current customers and target market as you simultaneously gather high-impact market intelligence and build stronger relationships.

How do you create an ongoing dialogue with your current customers and your target market? I have good news about that. I am going to let you sit in while two colleagues, both business persons like yourself, grill me on how you do this with surveys. Their names are Jim Loesch and Carter Harkins, and they are real people with real businesses. Carter Harkins is the CEO of Harkins Creative, a digital creative agency that helps companies identify and tell their Brand's Story. Jim Loesch shows local businesses how to take over their market by driving increased prospect flow using the latest Internet-based strategies.

You can sit back and enjoy the ride while they pick my brain mercilessly. At the end of each topic interview, I will give you a "Key Points Summary" so you will have the essence of the conversation at your fingertips. That will make it easier for you later when you are thinking about how you can use this strategy to take your company to new heights! In later chapters, I will share what you need to know to have the edge when you implement this strategy. At the end, I will provide an "Executive Summary" of the key points covered in the book. Let's get started!

Chapter Two

A Strategy That Creates Superior Competitive Advantage

"This strategy is broadly applicable, conceptually simple and has enormous potential return-on-investment."

Chapter Two
A Strategy That Creates Superior Competitive Advantage

Join Carter, Jim and me in a conversation about how strategically planned customer and market surveys can put your company on top.

The Benefits of Implementing Strategic Market Surveys

Carter: I have done surveys before and gathered the statistical data, but what you are saying is that if surveys are used creatively, I can build relationships. Is that the gist of where you are going?

Marie: Yes. That is exactly where I am going with this and, you know, one of the things that fascinates me, Carter, is that most businesses really do not have a concept of surveys as a vehicle for building relationships. They view surveys simply as a way to gather data from their customers or from the market at large. That is a very one-dimensional approach to surveys, which does not begin to tap the potential of a strategic survey to support business success.

There is an entirely different way to think about surveys and that is surveys as a dialogue, an ongoing conversation with your customers and your marketplace. When you approach surveys in that fashion, you are able to do a number of things simultaneously.

A. You are able to gather the market intelligence that you need. Examples might be your current customer satisfaction level, input about your products or your services, or information about how you compare to your competition. Or, you might be gathering information from the broader market place about the needs that they have. You can then explore meeting those needs with your product or service. These are the common uses of market and customer surveys.

B.   You can gauge changes in the desires, needs and wants of your customers and your marketplace over a period of time. You can do that by conducting a series of surveys over time, wherein you ask some of the same questions at intervals to the same target market or current customer group. Then you look at the answers to those questions over time, and you are able to discern market trends. You might want to do something like this when there has been a change in the market environment that might have changed your customers' needs. This allows you to stay abreast of changes in your marketplace, and that is very critical.

C.   You are able to strengthen your relationship with your current customers and create or strengthen the relationship with your target market. You do this through ongoing surveys that build on one another. One beauty of this is that you can gather your market intelligence in small manageable bites. This can work better for you and the people to whom you are asking questions. This helps with one of the challenges in gathering data, which is that there is a limit to the number of questions people are willing to answer.

D.   You get a double benefit if you use surveys as a relationship building strategy. As you build that relationship, people become more willing to answer more of your questions. This increases your ability to get more pertinent market intelligence at any time.

Another common application of surveys is to measure and improve current customer service satisfaction levels. It pays off handsomely in stronger customer relationships if you take action on what you discover and report to your customers in a timely manner what you are doing in response to their input.

You can use surveys to identify weaknesses and strengths in your customer service strategies and processes.   You can discover invaluable information about:

A.   Overall satisfaction with customer service levels

B.   Customer experiences in pre-sales processes

C.   Reasons for returns

D.   Your customers' experience on your website

E.   Any kind of interaction that you have with your customers

Jim: I have always heard that people will not do surveys. Is that not a barrier to implementing this strategy?

Marie: It is a myth that people will not do surveys. If that were true, none of the well-known polling companies would be in business. If you go online and search the word "surveys," you will be deluged with reports of survey results on many different topics. Are there some people who never answer surveys? Yes. All you need for this to work is enough people in your target market or current customer base, depending on the nature of your survey, who will answer it.

People Will Answer Surveys
If You Position and Conduct Them Effectively

Contrary to popular belief about surveys, many people actually enjoy giving their opinion, but this only holds true if they know that it is worth their time to do so. They have to understand what is in it for them. Reasons can include that they want to be helpful, influential or in the know. They cannot know that taking your survey will meet one of those needs unless you tell them. Sharing with them what you found out in the survey helps to meet all three of these needs. In general, people like to be helpful if you approach them correctly.

It is effective to say to people, "Will you help us?" when you ask them to answer a survey for you.

You must also manage their expectations about what is going to happen as a result of the information you have gathered. When they understand up front that you will be giving them feedback on what you find out, they are more likely to answer. This also taps into the curiosity factor with people and the competitive factor with some folks who like to be the ones who are "in the know."

When you are reaching out to your prospective customers, you can also offer some kind of incentive. It can be a product sample if that is workable for you in terms of cost and logistics. (Note: there are schools of thought that frown on this practice. You have to decide if it is right for your company and target market.) Generally, you do not want to offer something of such high value that people say they are willing to do the survey just to get the gift and then they respond with random answers on the survey to get through it quickly. On the other hand, you do want them to know how much you appreciate them. Put whatever you give them in context as a thank you gift, rather than a bribe.

The incentive can be something that you can deliver via computer, if your target market tends to be computer owners. A good choice in many situations like this is some kind of special report that contains information relevant to the need or want that your product or service is designed to meet. It must be valuable information, not a thinly disguised sales pitch, but you can always include information about how to contact you or view your product.

Your current customers will generally be willing to spend more time answering questions from you, because they already have a relationship with you. They can see the connection with the benefit to them if you make improvements in products or services that they already have or may buy from you in the future.

Carter: Something in the way you describe this suggests that there is more communication going on here than in the average survey situation. Could you address that?

Marie: That is exactly right. What makes this process so powerful is that it is two-way communication. You are, in essence, having a conversation with the people who are your current customers or your target market. That is why this works to build relationships. Another thing that makes surveys a vehicle for building relationships is giving information back to your survey respondents, whether to your market at large or to your current customers, as to what you found out.

Two-Way Communication Is Imperative

You do not want to have one-way communication, which is typically how companies do surveys. In most cases, businesses will put a survey out to their customers or their target market to gather data. Unfortunately, from the point of view of the people who gave the data, it went into a black hole somewhere. They never hear back from the business as to what it was that you discovered.

More importantly, they do not know what you are going to do as a result of the data, if anything. They do not know if you will respond by taking action that will result in serving them better. They do not feel that they made an impact or will benefit in some way for the time and effort they put in to giving the information. This is a major reason why many people resist taking surveys.

If you have something exciting to share as a result of what you discovered in your survey process, then share that. If you make some kind of commitment or announcement, then make sure that you deliver on what you said. In some cases, part of what you found out may be leading to a new product launch and you are not quite ready for that to be public knowledge. You must use some judgment about what you want to make public, but there is going to be plenty that you can share. You communicate back to the people you got the data from about what you discovered, what are you going to do about it and how that is going to help them.

Keep in mind that you are not trying to sell them anything at this point. You just want to let them know that you appreciate their input and that you actually did something with it. In summary, you need to:

- Ask questions to gather market intelligence

- Determine your key findings and decide on the appropriate course of action in response

- Communicate to your survey respondents and market at large, as appropriate, what you discovered and plan to do about it

- Ensure that you keep any commitments that you make

- Continue two-way communication

It is a Conversation!

Think of the process of building this relationship via surveys as a dialogue, which by definition is two-way communication. It is a conversation that you and your current customer or target market are having with some time lapses in between. One of the ways you keep that flow going, just as is true in a live conversation, is that you build on what came before. This works naturally and automatically because you ask a question and they respond. That raises more questions for you as the business owner, top management team, sales and marketing department, or customer service department.

Now, you may want to ask more questions to get clarity or more detail on their last input, or you might want to let them know you have a couple of ideas about how to address the needs or wants they told you about and you want their input about that. When they respond to those questions, it is going to bring up new issues or the desire for clarification on your part. You turn those topics into new, pertinent questions, and then you put those out to them.

You say something along the lines of, "Based on the last survey, here's what we discovered, and here's what we are wondering now. We'd like your help to fine-tune this so we can best meet your needs." Alternatively, you might say, "So that we can best understand what will serve you best." You will say whatever is appropriate, depending on the nature of the questions you are asking now, but always with the emphasis on the benefit to them.

Just remember, this is a conversation that you are having, just as though you were face-to-face with them. Admittedly, there are time lapses and more constraints on how many things you can "converse about" at one time. It is an elegantly simple concept. A dialogue allows you to do so many things. This applies equally to for-profits and non-profits. Basic human nature and needs are the key and that is the same regardless of who is involved.

People appreciate knowing that you really are trying to meet their needs and that you are willing to take the time and make the effort to communicate back to them. That puts more meaning into the relationship and it begins to make the customer, or the marketplace that you are dealing with, feel closer to your company or organization.

Carter: I would like to interject something here, if I may. Something you just said triggered a thought about how the kind of survey process that you are talking about mirrors a real conversation.

I know when I have a conversation with people, if it is obvious they have an agenda and they are marching through asking question after question, but not really taking into account any of the things that I have told them, I start to feel used. I start to feel that this is not a two-way discussion. This is somebody who is trying to march me to a conclusion that they want me to draw, or they have some other agenda.

However, when I am asked a question and I respond to it honestly, and then the next question that they ask acknowledges what I have just said, then I feel respected in the conversation. I feel that I have been heard and that I can then be even more honest with them in responding to the things that they are asking me. I become a participant. I willingly join the conversation to give them more of the feedback that they are after, because I can tell that they really care, they really listen. They are actually taking what I am saying into account and asking the next question, not because it is the next one on their list, but because it is the next question that makes sense.

It is that sort of relational, conversational approach that I understand you are suggesting with surveys. You are saying that the survey is the starting point to initiate dialogue. Through the dialogue, the customer, or the market that you are going to be operating in, starts to see that you are involving them in the process. They are not simply a fish in the pond that you are angling to get on the hook. They realize that you are really trying to have a dialogue with them about what their needs are and how you could meet those needs.

Then you are sharing with them what that new product might look like and how it would meet their stated needs, including what features it could have. These things let them know that they are now a part of the solution that you are going to create for them. It seems that you are suggesting that you progressively fine-tune your information gathering. You ask more penetrating questions in each successive survey on a particular topic. As a result, the customer starts to feel more and more appreciated and more and more involved in coming up with the very solutions that they really need.

Marie: That is a great summary. I could not have said it better myself. Another interesting thing about conceiving of this process as a dialogue is that you can turn written dialogue into interview dialogue. You can start out with a written survey and, as part of the process, ask people if they would be willing to take a phone call. If they say yes, then you ask for the phone number and give them a multiple-choice question of best times of day or evening to call them. You create one or more follow up questions you want to ask and then call them after you get the written surveys in.

In this case you can either make the written survey not anonymous, or you can let the written survey be anonymous (sometimes more people will answer in that case) and ask them to click on a link to a new page for an online form if they are interested in doing a later phone interview to discuss the topic further.

This takes more time than written surveys, but the interaction is much richer and you can get fantastic information this way. Most companies underutilize interviews or live conversations as a survey process. This is unfortunate, because they can be a very powerful way to get specific information from both your current and prospective customers that you will not get with other methods.

Do not get swept away by single inputs or small numbers of inputs. Your total survey sample needs to be large enough to get a reliable and representative picture of your population.

No matter how large your target market is, in most situations the maximum sample size you need is about 400 correctly completed responses to have an acceptable sample. If you want to see how the math works, just search on the Internet for the term "sample size calculator" and you will find plenty of free programs for doing this calculation.

However, this is only true if you obtain survey respondents in such a way that the people who choose to respond are a representative sample of your target market. Put another way, if you are fishing for trout, do not go to a fishing hole that predominantly has catfish to find your survey respondents. If you want to be able to sub-divide your respondents into demographic or other subcategories of your total responses for more in-depth analysis, then you will need a larger overall sample to ensure that your sub-groups are also of sufficient size to be acceptable samples.

It Is Essential to Focus on
Honoring and Serving Your Customer

You touched on something very important here and that is honoring people. Your motivation has to be customer centered. You must really want to help the people that you are in business to serve, no matter what your specialty is. It cannot just be about what is good for the business without balancing what is good for your customer, even when sometimes it is inconvenient for you.

Businesses know this, but sometimes they lose track of it. Chasing the dollar overwhelms focusing on what happens to their customer. In the long run, that never works out very well for anybody, not for their customer or their prospect nor for them as a company.

You know that it is critical to focus on what is genuinely good for your customers and to communicate in such a way that they know that is your focus. The question is, "How well are you doing it?"

How can you give more to your customer, add more value to the relationship and be respectful in the relationship?

Honest   transactions,   both   monetary   and   emotional,   are paramount. If what you are doing is mutually beneficial for your company and your customer, then it is easy to be transparent because you have nothing to hide. Honesty, transparency, genuine caring, discipline and consistency - these are all words that I associate with a successful business and a successful survey process.

Unless you were raised by wolves or have been living as a hermit on a mountaintop in Tibet all of your life, you have been in relationships with other human beings. Think about what those relationships were like. What did you want from the other people? What did the other people want? All of us want to be heard. We want to be valued. We want to be supported.

When your customer has that experience with you, they feel that they are in a relationship, and that makes them want to do business with you as long as their needs are being met in the relationship. When the product or service they need or want matters to them, they will not want to do business with somebody else even if somebody else is cheaper or closer. Strategic ongoing use of surveys gives you the platform to build this kind of relationship.

Jim: Are there any other advantages to the business in using this approach?

Marie: Yes, there are two additional points.

Surveys Are an Opportunity to
Share as Well as Collect Information

It gives the business an opportunity to build interest in something and to have a vehicle for a steady trickle of information going out to the market and current customers. It helps to keep your business "top of mind" with the customer. When they do need what you offer, they are much more likely to think of you. Keep in mind that the survey is not just an end in itself; it is a tool for having this dialogue. One of the things that you can do in a dialogue is give as well as receive information.

A good survey process is a platform for sharing information with your market and with your current customers on issues that they care about and that you want them to know about. It may be related to what you are working on in the survey dialogue. It may be a brief related message wherein you are using your survey as a vehicle to communicate about something else. An advantage is that you can use this as a low-key way to share information, especially to start building excitement about an upcoming product or service change.

This is why movies have 'coming attractions.' Movie producers want to get people excited about their film in advance so that they seek it out. As the saying goes, "people like to buy, but nobody likes to be sold." You pull them to you, instead of pushing things at them.

Since you are in an ongoing process with them, they are more likely to attend to your message than might otherwise be the case. In addition, as a bonus, remember that once you have built a relationship with them, they are more interested in attending to what you have to ask or say, as well as putting more credence in it.

You Are Qualifying Prospects for Your Product or Service

The fact that they answered your survey is what we might call, in marketing language, a hand raiser. They, in essence, raised their hand and said, "I'm interested in this issue." If they are not, they are not going to waste their time taking your survey. Therefore, you already know that the people who responded to your survey have a serious interest in the solution you might be able to offer. They are open to hearing more about how you might help with the problem or the opportunity that they are trying to address. Right away, you have done some degree of pre-qualifying and that is a terrific value to your company. Of course, you need to communicate with them when you do have a solution to offer for their issue.

Return on Investment with This Strategy

Jim: Would you address return on investment from this survey strategy?

Marie: As a manager or owner of a business, obviously you need to know if this strategy is worth doing. When you do the math, you will see that the potential impact on a company is likely to be quite significant. Think about your business. Estimate the possible percent impact on your sales of having an intimate knowledge of what your market will buy, coupled with a process that allows you to stay in touch with them meaningfully at regular intervals.

What if you had sales of $10,000,000 and this survey strategy made even a 1% improvement in sales? That is $100,000. One percent is an extremely conservative number for how much you are likely to be able to improve your sales. What you will get depends on your company and the marketplace, but you could get 5%, 10% or even much greater increases in sales. If your sales are $50,000,000, then a 1% increase in sales is $500,000. A 5% increase in sales is $2,500,000 or a 10% increase in sales is $5,000,000. Companies who get to know their target market intimately have even increased sales by as much as 300% as you will see in the story below.

Your results will vary based on many factors including how well and consistently you implement the survey strategy, especially taking action on what you learn. By what percent do you think you can improve sales if you uncover new key knowledge about your customers? Calculate your company's potential return on investment based on your sales and anticipated percent improvement.

Annual sales x Estimated percent of sales improvement as a result of implementing a strategic survey system to get much closer to your customers and prospects = Dollar amount of sales increase

Even if you use professional help to create the system and include the time of your own employees to implement it, your returns should amply justify the investment. One of the nice things about this strategy is that once you get the system in place, the overhead to maintain it does not increase as your sales increase.

Consider just one example (a real life story) of the impact of good market research on sales and profits. Imagine an exclusive fashion store in a wealthy suburb. The owner assumed the clientele was predominantly local and advertised accordingly in the local paper. She did not keep a customer mailing list because she felt it was unnecessary when they were virtually next door and she could easily reach out to them with the local media.

When she eventually did begin to survey her customers, she discovered that 66% of her customers lived 25 to 40 miles away! They came to shop at her store because they perceived that was where the fashion conscious crowd shopped. Based on this understanding of who her customers actually were and what their emotional motivations were, she changed her advertising strategy radically, including starting direct mail campaigns to those areas.

In six months, she tripled her business! Based on this true story, you can see that the example above of a 5% improvement could be very conservative. Even at that modest level, the payoff is substantial for a company. Imagine what it will be like if you get results even remotely approaching those obtained by the fashion store. Ask yourself these questions:

How much do you know about your customers and prospects?

Have you made some assumptions about who they are, where they are and what they want?

Do you know the commonalities shared by your customers that you could leverage in all areas of your business: sales and marketing strategies, product and service offerings, customer service delivery and other key areas?

You cannot run your business effectively if you are not crystal clear about exactly who your best customers and prospects are. Gathering and applying in-depth information about your target market is one of the most profitable things you can do for your business. Building a relationship at the same time is money in the bank.

Jim: There is a multiplying effect as well, because if you consider that this strategy not only addresses getting new customers but also retaining your current customers, the picture gets even better. You get more customers and then improve their loyalty, so they stay with you longer. The value of your customers multiplies. You are also more likely to be able to command a premium for your products and services since you match the market needs so well, which then adds another layer to the value. It is a multiplying effect all across the board. For a relatively modest investment, it really has the potential for a great return.

Final Thoughts on the Power of This Strategy

Carter: After talking with you and hearing more about this survey process, I certainly think this strategy is worth exploring and implementing. Ultimately, what I know in my business is that the value of the relationship is paramount. It is the thing that drives all the profit centers of my business. When I maintain that relationship, when I truly understand my clients' needs, then I will be able to generate a lot more sales and profits than I would otherwise.

I also like the systematic approach to asking questions and then gauging the next set of questions based on what I have just learned from my market or current customers.

Marie: Since you are a brand communication expert, Carter, I especially appreciate your thoughts on this strategy.

Jim: Do you have an opinion about this survey-based strategy in comparison to other strategies you have seen companies use to build their sales and profits?

Marie: That is a great question, Jim. Over the years, in the process of the strategic thinking and operational planning that I've done with clients and strategies I've helped them consider, there aren't many strategies I have found, seen, or helped to develop that are as broadly applicable, as conceptually simple and have the potential return-on-investment that this does.

Once you know how to do it, the more you do it, the easier it gets. The rewards are substantial, and it is not unduly expensive to implement. You have a methodology that you can use forever in multiple situations with both your current and prospective customers.

Key Points Summary

Market Survey Uses

- Gather market intelligence

- Gauge changes in market trends

- Strengthen customer relationships

- Build market relationships

- Measure customer satisfaction

- Evaluate customer service strategies and processes

- Give as well as collect information

- Create excitement about upcoming offerings

- Qualify prospects

Chapter Three

Get into the Heads and Hearts of Your Target Customers

"This strategy will work for you, whether your company is two people or two thousand people."

Chapter Three

Get into the Heads and Hearts
of Your Target Customers

There is a flow to implementing an ongoing survey process. We will explore the steps below to take in implementing this strategic survey system. You will simultaneously gather top-notch market intelligence and build high-impact relationships with your current and prospective customers.

Before you read this, let me caution you. There is a tendency to get overwhelmed when you read a list of things to do for any task. This is no exception. I am giving you as much information as I can to increase your understanding of this strategy and the full process.

You are in the driver's seat. You can choose to do this on whatever scale works for you. In later chapters, I will give you some examples of simple ways to do this. You can use this strategy whether your company is a few people, thousands of people or anything in between.

One Process for Implementing
Market Surveys in Your Company

These are the steps in one approach to doing a survey. We will consider preparation, implementation and follow-up.

Preparation

1. Establish the target market and objectives for the survey. Be clear about what you want to gain from each survey process.

2. Determine who needs to be on your survey project team, if you plan to use a team approach. You get two benefits from

using teams to work on your survey projects: input that is more comprehensive into the process and improved inter-departmental coordination (when that applies).

3. Decide how you are going to reach the people you want to take the survey (via letter, email, notice on website, etc.).

4. Pick a format and delivery method that works for this particular survey target and situation, for example, a mailed paper survey or an online survey or interviews.

5. Create a simple action plan with dates to manage your survey project and be sure to include the steps to analyze the data, decide on follow up actions to take and communicate what you found out.

6. Decide how many survey responses you need to get to have a reliable sample. Refer to page 35 for the discussion on this issue.

7. Decide whether you are going to offer a thank you gift for taking the survey, and if so, what it will it be and how you will deliver it. If you are using an online survey service, then a downloadable gift of some kind works well, because you already know that your survey respondents have access to a computer.

Implementation

8. Write your survey questions or obtain surveys already created for your type of situation and then customize them.

9. Decide whether you are going to do some interviews with a sample of your target market. If so, develop a small number

of questions that you would like to pursue in more detail
with your market, and use those in your interviews. In this
process, you may also get input that suggests additional
questions for your survey or the best way to tailor the
existing questions to your situation.

You can also conduct interviews as a follow up to a written
survey, if you want to explore something in more detail,
related to the written survey results.

10. Pre-test your survey with a small group from your target
    market, to be sure your questions and instructions are clear.
    This is always recommended, even if you use pre-written
    surveys obtained from experts, as each target market has a
    different perspective.

11. Distribute the surveys.

12. Collect responses.

13. Analyze the data.

Follow-up

14. Decide on what action to take in relation to what you have
    discovered.

15. Create an action plan for implementation.

16. Communicate your findings both within your company and,
    as appropriate, depending on the nature of the information,
    back to those who responded to the survey or to your market
    at large. This establishes the dialogue that you want to
    continue with your customers and your target market.

17. Decide what you want to explore next via survey and continue the process. Remember, it is a dialogue, not a single event. Treat it that way and you get great market and customer intelligence and build relationships at the same time.

Here are some tips on how to address step one above, which is to establish your survey objectives and your target market for each survey you decide to do. *You must do this step well, in order to successfully implement this strategy.*

Establish Your Objectives for Each Survey

To determine your survey objectives, ask yourself, "What benefit for the company do we want to get out of this survey?"

A. Test satisfaction with customer service levels?

B. Get a fix on overall market wants and needs?

C. Get input on a specific product or service that we are considering offering?

D. Get input from current customers so that we can improve current products or services?

Now, in this order, ask yourself:

1. What topics do we want to explore?

2. Exactly what kind of information are we seeking?

3. What do we hope to do with the information that we get?

4. When the project is finished, what do we expect to have gotten out of this? If you are not clear about this, you cannot structure your questions correctly.

5. If we do get the information and understanding that we want from this survey, what practical difference will that make to our business results?

Who Is Your Target Market For Each Survey?

Ask yourself the following questions, in this order:

1. Who is the target market that this survey is focused on?

2. Based on our objective for the survey and the list of topics we plan to cover, who has the best knowledge, perspective or experience to give us quality, informed information and opinions about our chosen topic?

3. Whom do we want to reach with this survey - current customers, prospective customers in this target market or both?

4. What characteristics are shared by our target market for this survey? (These are variables such as location, age, gender, race, problem to be solved, interests, what publications they read, whom they consult for advice, where they congregate and any other factor pertinent to what you want to explore.)

5. Write a summary statement that describes clearly whom you want to reach with this survey.

Key Points Summary

**The Basics of Implementing
the Strategic Market Survey Cycle**

1. Establish the target market and objectives for the survey.
2. Decide how you are going to reach the people you want to take the survey (via letter, email, notice on website, etc.).
3. Pick a format and delivery method for the target market.
4. Decide how many survey responses you need to have a reliable sample.
5. Decide whether you are going to offer a thank you gift for taking the survey, and if so, what it will it be and how you will deliver it.
6. Create an action plan with dates to manage your survey project.
7. Create your survey.
8. Decide whether you are going to do interviews with a sample of your target market before the written survey to get input for your questions or after to explore in more detail your written survey findings.
9. Pre-test your survey with a small group from your target market.
10. Distribute the surveys and collect responses.
11. Analyze the data.
12. Decide on what action to take in relation to what you have discovered and create an action plan for implementation.
13. Communicate your findings, both within your company and back to those who responded to the survey or to your market at large.
14. Decide what you want to explore in your next survey and continue the process. Remember, it is an ongoing dialogue.

Chapter Four

Turbo-Charge Your Existing
Customer Relationships
to Drive Higher
Sales and Profits

"When you ask the right questions, analyze the responses and take action, it will pay off handsomely. When you do it repeatedly, it will pay off beyond your wildest dreams."

Chapter Four

Turbo-Charge Your Existing Customer Relationships to Drive Higher Sales and Profits

Carter: If a company wants to use the survey process to learn more about their existing customers and strengthen that relationship, how do they get started? What advice would you have for them?

Marie: I would love to address that. Here are the first questions companies need to ask themselves:

1. In what ways do we presently gather data from our current customers?

2. Do we have any kind of structured, ongoing process for this beyond what customers say when they call customer service because they have an issue?

3. Do we collect data on our customer service calls so that we know that in a given week, month, or quarter that we had X number of calls and that a certain percentage of them were about issue A and a certain percent were about issue B and so forth?

4. What is critical for us to know about the experience of our customers with us?

5. In what areas, pertinent to our business, do we need to know more about the needs, wants, desires and fears of our customers?

6. What creates competitive advantage in our industry?

7.   What, related to that, do we need to know from, or about, our customers? In our company's specific experience, do we have any information about what has resulted in getting more customers or losing customers in the last twelve months?

Summarize What You Know and Need to Find Out

Whether you are a small company with just a handful of people and everyone has multiple jobs, or a larger company with hundreds or thousands of employees and hundreds of millions in sales, I encourage you to sit down and discuss these questions.

However you go about it, someone representing the departments responsible for customer service, sales and marketing, product design and a representative of top management need to be involved.

You may be surprised at what surfaces when you focus on this, especially with multiple inputs. In some companies, one of the things that surfaces is that departments have information that other departments need, but there has been no coordination or sharing of that information. In other cases, there is duplicate effort that is wasting resources.

Now you have a list of all the ways in which you currently are gathering data, whether it is because you are reaching out to the customers in some fashion or they are coming to you and you are tabulating the results of the input that you receive over time.

You also have the beginning of a list of areas for which you are lacking adequate information. You have made a start at answering the question: "What is it that we need to find out from our customers?" Note that this is not just a tactical exploration. It is an important strategic conversation.

Make It Manageable

Reduce it to something manageable. Look at which issues are most important now, either because you need to address them quickly or because they have critical strategic implications. The 80/20 rule is a good approach. What 20% of the things that you said you needed to explore about your customers will have an 80% impact on your business? Separate those and then, if need be, ask the 80/20 question repeatedly until you get a topic to explore that is a manageable, productive place to start your survey process.

Now brainstorm this question. "What are 3 to 10 questions that we could ask about this issue or area to start this dialogue with our current customers?" Do not try to get all the information about the issue at once. You do not know which way this conversation with your customer is going to unfold, so get a piece at a time and then pursue that further with them. This keeps the conversation going and makes the process manageable for you and your customers. They are not likely to want to answer 20 questions right off, so start small. As they get involved and interested, you will be able to ask more of them.

Getting to Customers

Now ask, "What is the easiest way to get this to our customers?" It depends upon what your customer communication channels are. If you have email addresses for all of your customers and your experience has been that they get the emails you send and actually open them, that is one alternative. Whatever you do, figure out the best way to get to them that is workable for both you and them. Do keep in mind that in this digital age, most people are comfortable with computer-based approaches.

Many excellent and inexpensive online survey services are available that make it easy for you to put a survey on a website and then just send a link to it. Online-based surveys are much more common today than paper surveys. Another advantage of this is that they include programs to tabulate results for you.

If you are in one of those rare situations in which your customers do not have computer access, then you may have to survey the old-fashioned way, on paper with surveys that you mail with a stamped, self-addressed envelope, which they mail back to you. You can also send out scannable forms that are machine read. The data is automatically entered into a scoring program. You can do in person interviews, especially if you have a storefront. You can also do phone interviews, which is especially workable with current customers. Since they already have a relationship with you, they can see a potential benefit to them from talking to you.

Now, put together a simple action plan that lays out what you are going to do, by when (refer back to Chapter 3 for the steps in the process) and who is responsible for each step.

The Importance of a Strategic Mindset

If, in the course of having the conversation suggested above, you cannot get answers that you feel confident about, then you need to look to your own strategic thinking and current operations. If you cannot answer those questions, your company is in danger of making mistakes that will be likely to cost you customer loyalty and market share.

It is critical that you approach the whole issue of relationship building and market/customer intelligence gathering with a strategic mindset. Implementing it is an operational task, but it is a strategic issue to build competitive advantage. It is strategic to build long-term customer loyalty so that people do not even want to think about going anyplace else. It is important to have the whole survey conversation in the context of, "Where do we intend to go as a company over the long haul, and how will this serve us in doing that?" You definitely do not want to confine yourself to dealing only with operational issues, such as customer service issues.

Once you get into the habit of regularly thinking and acting about this strategically, as well as operationally, you will create competitive advantage. Here are some more tips on how to think strategically about your survey process.

Integrating the Market Survey with Your Strategic Direction

As companies, we often believe that we know what our customers and our markets want and need, and in some cases we do to a significant degree. But, it is also true that virtually always when we ask them, we discover something new, or we discover that we have some misunderstanding or erroneous assumption about our current customers or target market. It is important to consider your current customers in the context of your total strategic direction and target market.

A Brief Exercise in Strategic Thinking and Surveys

1. Review your strategic plan or formulate your strategic direction if you have not done that before.

2. Conduct a strategic thinking session with your executive team to review your strategic direction.

3. Make lists of the target markets you are addressing, products and services you currently have or are planning and the competition that you are concerned about.

4. Now make a list of all the things you would like to know more about related to these areas.

5. Then consider how a series of carefully focused surveys could help you get the market and competitive intelligence you need.

Carter: What if a company does not have a lot of people and resources? How can they approach this so that it is manageable?

Marie: That is a question many people have.

How You Can Simplify the Process of Connecting with Your Current Customers if You Are a Smaller Company

For smaller companies, implementing an ongoing strategic survey process may seem too hard, too complicated and too time consuming. That does not have to be the case. You can scale the survey process to fit whatever resources you have. You can approach this very simply by starting off with just one question that you ask your current customers. Most people do not think of that as a survey. When you say survey, companies tend to envision many questions that will take a lot of time and effort to prepare and analyze, but you can begin your survey process with just a few questions or even a single question.

Remember, it is a conversation, not a single event, so you can start the ball rolling with one question and then let it unfold from there. You can keep doing single or a few questions at a time indefinitely if that works best for your customers and your company.

All you have to do is determine, "What's the most important question you could ask right now?" Refer to the process outlined above for deciding what to pursue. Here are a few additional questions that you can ask yourself if those above do not do it for you.

1. What is the customer related issue that we most need better information about so that we can make better decisions for running the business?

2. What is the issue that is causing us, as a company, the most problems right now? Are we lacking some information or understanding about it that we could gain by asking a few questions to our customers?

Get Creative with the Survey Process

Do you have a storefront? You may have seen stores that have a computer where you can take a brief survey. Another approach is to have one question you want to ask and ask it as people purchase, or you have someone in the store who goes up to people and asks if they will speak with him or her for a minute. You are limited only by your imagination in the number of ways you can access your customers and open your survey dialogue with them.

Consider the nature of your business. How long do people stay there? If they are only going to be in your business for 10 minutes, then you might ask one simple, multiple-choice question on paper that they can do in 15 seconds while waiting to check out.

If you have a restaurant and they are going to be there for an hour, you have an opportunity for them to take a short survey. You could train your wait staff to have a pre-printed survey card and say to their customer table, "We want to find ways to serve you even better. Could you help us by completing this short survey?" If they say yes, you give a card to each person at the table, perhaps along with a complimentary pen with your restaurant's name on it. You ask them to fill it out while they are waiting and offer a complimentary beverage as a thank you. The card may have two or three multiple choice questions and one narrative (open-ended) question. The average person can do this in a lot less time than it takes their meal to come. It is easy, quick and inexpensive to do this way.

What if you do not have customers sitting in your establishment for an hour? Okay. You might have someone stationed at the exit to your store doing short interviews, in which they ask the questions and fill out the answers for people on the card.

You might decide to do telephone interviews. You can ask permission of the people who come into your storefront to call them later. If they agree, then you ask for their contact information and the best time to call them. You might send written communication to your customer list asking for volunteers. If your customers routinely come to your website, it is easy to set up the survey online and offer them an inducement to take it.

These are a few examples of how you can be creative in engaging your current customers. You can think of equally creative ways to do this in your business. If you ask the right questions, analyze the responses and then take action, it will pay off handsomely. If you do this repeatedly, it will pay off beyond your wildest dreams.

The possibilities are endless. Ask yourself, "How can we be creative in engaging our current customers?" Decide which of the many survey strategies that your business has discussed is the best fit for your company now. Then determine your next steps.

Make it fun. People respond better to fun. Companies have done creative things like send out a briefcase, and to get the combination to the lock the person had to take the survey. Obviously this is a fairly expensive approach and only appropriate for limited situations, but the idea of making it fun can be applied to most situations. For example, you could create some kind of treasure hunt or contest or game with the survey embedded as a step in that process. The bottom line is that not only do you need to make clear what the benefit to answering the survey is for your potential respondents, but also make it fun as well if you can. It makes it more appealing for people to participate and increases the likelihood that they will. You do not have to do something like this every time, and there may be situations in which it would not be a good fit, but at least consider the "fun option", when appropriate.

Remember, this is an ongoing process. Once you have determined why you are doing it and what you need to get out of it, then you only have to decide on the first survey you are going to do with your customers. You do not have to know, in advance, everything about where you are going to take the process next. It is a living process, and what you ask in step two or five or ten of having this conversation is going to be based, at least in part, on the step that just preceded it. You might very well go in a different direction than you had initially imagined once the dialogue unfolds.

Maintaining the Process is Critical

Jim: Is there anything else that is critical to doing this successfully with your current customers?

Marie: Yes, one critical thing is to make a real commitment in your company to using surveys as a tool for an ongoing dialogue. A company needs to make a specific person accountable for managing this process and keeping the conversation going. You need this to be "somebody's baby" or put another way, you need a champion for this process. He or she is responsible for ensuring that you actually implement an ongoing strategic survey process and that once you get the information, you are proceeding with follow-up communication to the people who gave it to you. He or she has to ensure that at each step along the way, you actually do something with the data you collect. You do not want to drop the ball on implementation. Get started with baby steps if that is what you need to do. *Consistency is the key.* You do not have to do something complicated or expensive.

You do not have to be intimidated by this process. It scales beautifully and easily to exactly what you need it to do and how much resource you can bring to it. There is no excuse not to do this and every reason to do it. If you want higher sales and profits, competitive advantage and raving fan customers, then get started on this – the sooner, the better!

Key Points Summary

A Strategic Survey Process

- Evaluate current data gathering practices

- Brainstorm survey focus possibilities

- Use the 80/20 rule to narrow down the possibilities

- Determine what questions to ask

- Scale survey process to your needs and resources

- Start with just one question if need be

- Decide how to reach your desired survey respondents

- Do it! Analyze the data

- Decide action based on findings

- Communicate discovery and plans to your participants, customers or target market

- Take the action and communicate again

- Decide what you want to explore next

- Repeat the process with next question(s)

- Continue the cycle

Chapter Five

Ensure That Your
New Product or Service
Is Super Profitable

"If you involve your target market at every step along the way, listen to what they say and act on it, when you launch your new offering, customers with be lining up with their money in hand."

Chapter Five

Ensure That Your New Product
or Service Is Super Profitable

Jim: Could you talk a bit about using surveys when you are considering bringing out a new product or service? I know that this is an area of considerable risk for companies and I would like to hear your thoughts on how the survey process can help minimize that risk.

Marie: Development and launching of a new product or service is a primary use of market surveys because you have to know your market for that product or service intimately if you want to hit a home run with your new offering. You may discover that your market does not want the product that you were considering, or wants it, but at an unworkable price point. The time to find out that the marketplace is not interested in the product you have in mind, or is interested, but unwilling to pay the price point that makes the product profitable, is before you embark on actually developing and producing that product. This alone will help to make you successful when other businesses waste time and money because they fail to do their due diligence.

One good way to use surveys in this situation is to conduct a series of surveys to get the different types of information you need in this situation, in which each survey has a specific theme. We will explore that in a bit more detail.

Using Multi-Survey Campaigns

You do this by sending out a series of surveys to the same target population. The survey topics build logically, one after the other. You are therefore able to collect a substantial amount of information related to your proposed new product or service in short, manageable surveys. Here is an example of the flow of five surveys that you can do, listed in the suggested order for your campaign. *Do not do these unless you have first explored your target market's core needs, desires and fears*, as we discussed earlier. That is the foundation you must have in place before you get into the issues indicated in these five surveys.

Survey #1 is designed to clarify how strongly your target market feels about several factors related to a product or service. It allows you to determine what level of importance your target market places on each factor when making a buying decision about your particular type of product or service. Factors for consideration include the quality of the product, the price, confidence in the brand, the features that the product offers and how easy the product is to use.

Once you have a handle on this, then in Survey #2, you are ready to get some initial input about product design. You specifically want to include what features you already think, or know, are important to your target market for the particular kind of product or service you are considering. You want to uncover what features are most important to them, as well as what they typically dislike about this kind of product or service.

In Survey #3, you can refine your research about product features by taking the input that you received in the last survey, coupling it with other research results and experience with this product type, and use all that input to create a list of the features that you are now actively considering to include in your product. You then send this survey to the same list or whatever distribution channel you used as in the previous two surveys. At the time that you send this survey, you might indicate that if this product is produced, they will receive advance notice of its release as well as special consideration, such as a discount or bonus item, as a thank you for their interest and participation in its development. This, of course, requires that you obtain contact information from your respondents.

In Survey #4, you most likely want to get a feel for product pricing. If you did not offer the advance notice and special consideration promise in your last survey, this next survey would be a good time to do that.

By this time, you have collected data on multiple variables associated with development of this particular product. There are certainly other considerations unrelated to your market research, specifically including production, legal, and other aspects; but by now you should have a pretty good idea whether or not you should seriously consider this product further based upon your market's input.

In Survey #5, you explore issues with your prospective buyers to determine what their interest level would be in purchasing this product. This would be another opportunity to make a special offer.

Five surveys may seem overwhelming for you or for your respondents, but remember these things:

1. In this strategy of surveys as an ongoing dialogue, you want to be doing surveys routinely over time. Once you set up the system and get accustomed to it, you will not find it hard to do.

2. Each survey is short, usually from 3 to 15 questions, which can easily be done by your respondents in 5 minutes in most cases.

3. You will not do these all at once.

4. You will manage the expectations of your respondents by letting them know at the end of each survey that you will be back in touch and why. Then you will share appropriate feedback with them about what you found out and use that as the introduction to the next survey. Think of it as telling a story wherein they become curious about what will be in the next installment.

Here is a summary of the focus of the five surveys you can use in sequence in a new product or service development scenario. Keep in mind that in this situation, while you should be asking your current customers, you also definitely want to ask your larger target market.

You may also choose to combine surveys and do fewer of them. You will determine this by how important it is for you to know the answers to the last survey in order to ask the best questions in the next one. For instance, based on the list below you would want to do Surveys #2 and #3 separately because the answers from #2 will determine what you include in #3. You could potentially combine the first two into one survey and the last two can also be one survey.

Just a reminder, it is critical that you first understand the core need, desire and fear around the specific issue that your product or survey will address. You do not want to get into details about the product until you have that understanding. Then you can proceed with a series such as the five surveys outlined here:

Survey #1: Determine what level of importance your target market places on each factor when making a buying decision about your particular type of product or service

Survey #2: Uncover what product or service features are most important to them, as well as what they typically dislike about this kind of product or service (after first determining core issues)

Survey #3: Refine your research about product features

Survey #4: Explore product pricing

Survey #5: Ask your prospective buyers what their interest level in purchasing this product would be

Jim: How do you determine what questions to ask on your survey, specifically when you are surveying your target market and not your current customers?

Marie: There are several ways to handle this including hiring a professional in this area or finding a survey on the topic you need that has already been created so that you can tailor it for your own use. Those are available on the Internet at many of the survey hosting services. You can also find survey "how to" products that include prepared surveys.

Another approach that companies often miss is the advantage of doing some pre-interviews to get input for what kind of questions you should ask on your survey. You develop an initial set of questions based on what you already know you want to get input on from your target market. Then you assemble a small group of people who are representative of your target market and interview them to explore further. You can do it on the telephone.

It does not take a lot of interviews from your target market to gather enough input so that you can be sure that you have not missed some major choice you should have included in the multiple-choice answers on the survey. The good news about multiple-choice questions is that the data is very easy to analyze. The bad news is that even if you include the "Other" response choice, some people will not think of that or will not stop to fill something in if they have got a different idea.

If there is some major choice that the majority of your market would have checked if it had been there that you did not know to include, then you have a gap in your understanding of what is important to the market. I have done projects in which during the course of pre-interviews, a major new idea popped up that the company had never considered, so I know that this is important.

Let me tell you a story. I recall doing a complete survey campaign for a client who was working on a new product launch. I asked them questions to determine how well they already knew their target market and how they had concluded what needed to be covered in their survey about the product features and benefits.

They had a fairly good grasp of this, but it seemed to me that there were some holes in it. I suggested that I prepare a list of interview questions, based on what they thought needed to be included on their survey, and then they could interview a few dozen people to check that out.

I asked whether they had a good email list. It happened that they had an extensive prospect database of people who had asked for information through their website. I constructed an email inviting people to be interviewed, offered a sample product gift from my client company (with their blessing of course) and promised the interview would only take 10 minutes. You would be surprised how much territory you can cover in 10 minutes, if you are well organized.

I printed multiple copies of the interview questions with room to take notes and waited to see what kind of response we got to the offer. We were deluged. We received so many responses; we had to turn people away. Of course, you always want more people responding than you ultimately want to interview, since some will not be available when you call.

The interview process was an eye opener. There was one particular question for which many people offered the same response. It had not been included in what the client thought people would say. As a result, I added that to the actual survey we sent as one of the multiple choice answers for that topic.

When we had the responses, I was curious as to what percentage of people picked that answer in that multiple-choice question. It turned out to be one of the most frequently selected choices. Without the interview, we would have missed it unless a lot of people wrote it in under the "Other" response choice, but that would have been unlikely.

Even more interesting were peoples' responses overall while interviewing them. Many made comments indicating that the questions made them think about the issue in a new way. Several commented that they really enjoyed the interview process. Some commented how nice it was that the company cared enough to take the time to do interviews. As with many aspects of survey implementation, you can get multiple benefits from each aspect of the process. You are able to really leverage your time and resources.

In a new product development situation, you never know when you are going to discover something unexpected. You can have ideas about how the product should be, what the price point should be and so forth. But if you go to production and then to market without checking that with your market and your current customers first, the market will be glad to teach you a lesson the hard way. In the absence of good market input, you are very much at risk of investing your resources to develop something that the market is lukewarm about.

Questions to Consider When You Are
in a New Product Development Scenario

Who needs to be involved in giving input, possibly including suppliers, distribution channels and employees as well as current customers and your target market?

What are the deepest wants, needs, fears or desires of your target market in relation to this product or service?

What are the product related variables that are important enough to make the buy/no-buy decision for them?

What are the ones that do not matter at all?

Which variables are in the "nice-to-have" category somewhere in the middle?

Your customers are not going to come knocking at your door if your product does not address their needs, wants, desires and fears. Having a lot of nifty features that you thought would be great, but that are low on their priority list, never makes up for the mismatch, if you are not on target with what matters to them most

New product or service development is an excellent opportunity to engage in dialogue via surveys with your target market, current customers and others. The answers to questions that you ask are going to raise new questions to ask.

What you are doing is getting your customers into a partnership with you. They are helping you design the product. All of us have more investment in a decision in which we participate. (That is why companies put so much emphasis on participative management and teamwork.) As a result, the prospects and customers involved in your survey process are intrigued about the product.

When the Ford Motor Company first launched the new Taurus many years ago, they had the most successful new car model launch in the history of the industry up until that time. They experienced this success because they involved their dealers, their dealers' customers, their employees and their suppliers.

They asked each of those groups for input about the new model. They discovered things that were not going to work, based on supplier input. They discovered features that their customers really wanted. They got their employees and their dealers excited and engaged, as well as getting great input from them.

When the situation calls for it, seriously consider "casting a wider net" and involving everyone who has a role or a stake in your new product or service venture. You will be glad you did!

Benefits from Surveys in the Product Development Situation

One of the great things about this process is that you get multiple benefits. When you use an ongoing survey process in the new product or service development situation, you:

- Get the market intelligence you need

- Create the product or service that the market really wants and will pay for

- Build the participants' curiosity, just by the nature of the process, so you get the "coming attraction" curiosity

- Build their stake in the product or service, because they have been involved in the process, so they feel some ownership

Now, what do you suppose happens when you get ready to launch the product, you have been doing this with them all along, and now you tell them, "We are going to launch the product at this point in time. Thank you for your tremendous help along the way. We are going to give you advance notice and VIP treatment as a token of our appreciation. No one else will be getting everything that is included for our VIP's." You specify what you will be giving them or you send out the first message as a teaser to keep them interested and then subsequently announce what the VIP treatment will include. This might be a discount or something else of value, such as a warranty extension, product upgrade, bonus item, etc.

It is important in this situation to be certain that what you give for VIP's really does include something extra that no one else is getting in other offers, such as introductory specials, etc. Failure to really make the VIP treatment special will come back to haunt you when, inevitably, your VIP customers find you out. In any case, as a reputable, caring company, you do not want to engage in marketing ploys that are fundamentally lies.

People love being influential, being "in the know," being valued, being treated specially or getting a great deal. When you cover all these bases, involving your current customers and target market, people are going to be lining up, with their money in hand, when you come out with the new product or service for which they gave input. It does not get any better than that. To summarize very briefly what we have been discussing here:

- Discover what your market wants, needs, desires and fears
- Involve your market throughout the exploration process
- Create curiosity and a sense of ownership
- Get your market eager to buy

Jim: Yes, I think the whole process is so exciting. You are finding out exactly what they want. You are creating it and then presenting it to the market, and they go, "That is perfect!" or "That is me!" so they are going to buy it, because it is who they are and it is what they want.

Marie: Exactly right. All of your market with a need for that product or service, including the people who were not involved in the survey process, is going to have that reaction when you have correctly designed for what your market needs.

Key Points Summary

**Strategic Survey
New Offerings Exploration Process**

- Consider involving a broader audience with questions appropriate for each of them, such as distribution channels, employees, and suppliers in addition to your current customers and target market

- Consider multi-survey campaigns with your customers and target market, especially where input will drive new questions

- Use interviews to uncover additional questions to ask or to clarify input received in written surveys

- Create curiosity about "coming attractions"

- Build survey participants' emotional involvement and sense of ownership in the new offering

- Consider special deals at product or service launch for those who participated in your survey process

Chapter Six

Be the 800 Pound Gorilla in Your Target Market

"Discover exactly what will give you the competitive edge and get it!"

Chapter Six

Be the 800 Pound Gorilla
in Your Target Market

Linking Customer Surveys and Competitor Analysis
To Create Competitive Advantage

Carter: Can you address using surveys to create competitive advantage?

Marie: Let me tell you a story. I had a client that I was doing strategic thinking and planning work with. We were in the market research phase of the process and I said to them, "How do you stack up to your competition in relation to the key services that your customers expect in your particular industry?" They replied that they thought they stacked up really well. I replied, "Well okay, do you have any data on that?" They had some, but not enough. I said, "Okay, let's brainstorm a list of all the services, features and functions that your customers tell you they want." The entire top management team came up with a list.

I said, "Okay, now let's survey your customers, and let's do it around how important the things on this list are to them." Contrary to what they had believed, we discovered there was one major service that they did not provide, which their customers were quite upset about. They had been hearing complaints about this, but they had not realized how serious it was. "That'll be too expensive for us to do," and so forth. I said, "let's find out how you stack up to your competition on these services."

We did a competitive analysis, and what they discovered was that they were the only major player in their industry and locale who did not provide that one service that their customers were complaining so vehemently about.   They were shocked.   No wonder their customers were complaining.   The customers could get that service from any competitor who sold a similar item, but they could not get it from this particular company who, in many other respects, was superior in terms of ethics, customer service and product.

They did a little more research with their customers about what they wanted.   Then they looked for a cost-effective way to add that particular service, because otherwise they would continue to be at a competitive disadvantage.

What Are the Lessons We Can Learn from This Story?

- Never make assumptions about your competitive position

- Do not assume that customers are complaining unreasonably; if they are unhappy, you need to find out why

- Coordinate surveying your current customers with a competitor analysis for full benefits from both processes

- Be willing to make changes when you uncover compelling evidence that you are at a significant competitive disadvantage

Jim: How can you use the survey process to sway customers over to you from your competition?

Use the Survey Process to Sway Customers Over
To You from Your Competition

Marie: What drives market surveys in this direction is the nature of the questions that you ask the participants. In this scenario, you want to ask questions that have to do with how you are perceived in relation to your competition.   This is a place where narrative questions can be helpful, because it can be difficult to discern up front what kind of choices to put in multiple-choice questions.

Here are some examples of questions you can ask. "Have you ever done business with our competition?" (Yes or No) The next question you ask is "Please list their names here." If you are in a well-defined local market and the competition can all be listed, then you can say, "Please check any of the following that you have previously done business with" (where you provide a multiple-choice list of those companies).

With this information in hand, you have a better idea of where they are coming from; based on which competitors they have had experience with. Now you ask, "Have you done business with our company?" (Yes or No) If yes, then "When was the last time you did business with us?" (You provide multiple choices of time frames.) You ask this because you need to know how fresh their experience with you is.

Then you could ask, "How would you rate us in comparison to our competitors listed above?" (Provide multiple choices of approval levels.) Then you ask an open-ended question. "Please tell us the most important reasons for your rating above."

These are just some examples of how you can proceed. Which questions you ask, in how much detail and how many you ask will vary depending on each company's situation. You can see from these questions that you can get powerful information if you ask the right questions to the right people.

Once you understand what they like about you, you can capitalize on that by featuring it and communicating about it. Conversely, you can correct anything important that makes you less appealing than your competition and then communicate about what you now offer that is new.

You might ask the kinds of questions in the example above in general market research or you can focus on a single product or service, either current or under consideration. In that case, you phrase your questions accordingly so that they are focused on that one thing, instead of your general market position.

In that situation, you might ask your survey participants "Is there any way in which X kind of product or service provided by the companies named above (in the survey) is better than our product of the same type?" You might focus on a particular feature or benefit of the product that you want to explore.

You can ask a narrative question focused on a particular service type that you and your competition both offer in which you request them to compare you.

Alternatively, you can ask this kind of question "Is there anything that you particularly value that we offer in product Z or service X, which the other companies above do not offer?" A good follow up question to that is something like this: "What is important to you about the item you listed in the question above?"

The bottom line is that you have endless ways you can go with this. Pick one and take the process one-step at a time. See where it leads you.

Key Points Summary

How to Create
Sustainable Competitive Advantage

- Never make assumptions about your competitive position

- Do not assume customers are "whining" with no reason

- Coordinate surveying current customers with a competitor analysis

- Make changes when you uncover an important competitive disadvantage

- Identify your competitive strengths and weaknesses

- Capitalize on and communicate about your strengths

- Address your key weaknesses and, if possible and desirable to make them strengths, do so and then communicate that strength to your market

Chapter Seven

Connecting with
Your Customers
When Trouble Strikes

*"More than ever before, people do business
with companies who treat them fairly and
routinely demonstrate their good faith."*

Chapter Seven

Connecting with Your Customers
When Trouble Strikes

Carter: It occurs to me as we have been talking that a survey might actually be a good way for a company to be transparent with their customers when something major goes wrong, to own the catastrophe, so to speak. They could potentially do a lot of damage control and salvage those relationships that might otherwise be lost to them if their customers or markets do not understand what is going on. Talk to me a little bit about how surveys can be used in that context to help salvage relationships and make a bad situation better.

Marie: The answer to that is something that you just mentioned and that is transparency. The key is not hiding out and ducking the bad stuff. You can think of situations in corporate America in which companies have handled serious problems differently. Some stepped up to do the right thing by their customers or the larger community and others tried to "sweep things under the rug."

Because of the scandals in corporate America in recent years, people are more sensitive than ever before about honesty. They really pay attention to whether or not companies are doing what is best for the people they serve, or just doing what is best for them regardless of any negative impact. Health, safety and the environment are obvious topics.

Customers are also very alert to the claims that companies make about the functions and benefits of what they sell. They will not accept excuses, or even legitimate reasons, for serious product flaws if companies will not make things right once they do discover a problem.

The challenge for companies is in doing what is right for the greater good and for their customers, while simultaneously balancing their responsibility to the stockholders and others with financial vested interest in the company.   In doing this balancing act, involving the people who are impacted can be very helpful to all concerned.

In matters of safety, companies know that they must advise their customers or risk legal action and loss of reputation when things come to light. However, in other areas, there is a lot of latitude about what to address. Some companies are only straightforward when they think they have to be, whereas others operate from a strong value of putting the customer and what is morally right first, no matter how inconvenient or costly in the moment it might be.

One of the most classic examples of this was the Tylenol scare many years ago in which there were several incidents of bottles of Tylenol being tampered with. It could have been a very small number of the people who bought the product who would have run into a problem. Some outside agent caused the situation, not something in the manufacturing process.

Nevertheless,   Johnson   &   Johnson   responded   virtually instantaneously. They took the product out of stores, even though that cost them a great deal of money. They did not beat around the bush. They made an announcement about what was happening and what they were doing about it before rumors and panic could get much traction. In this situation, there was no need to consult with their customers. The solution and best protection for their customers was obvious to J&J.

They did the right thing and the goodwill that they built as a result was priceless. Their bottom line reflected that when they brought Tylenol back with protective packaging. They put out a clear message to the public that the safety of their customers came first. As a result, people had even more faith in the company and all their products. It confirmed in people's minds that J&J was the kind of company that they could trust.

However, there are many situations when it is not an issue of health and safety, wherein companies have many choices in how they can respond. In these situations, there is not just one right answer. There are many possible ways to go, each with their own pros and cons.

Since people want honesty, they want a company to say, "We've discovered this issue that could affect you." A company can use this as an opportunity to build even closer customer relationships. They can say something like, "We intend to address this issue as quickly and effectively as possible, and we need your help to do that."

This is where using a survey can come into play. The company can use it as a channel to not only find out what questions and concerns people have about the issue, but also to share information so as to prevent confusion, misunderstanding and concern.

They can offer a choice of solutions when that is possible and ask what those affected would prefer. If it is a problem with a current product or service people want to know, "How are you going to take care of me now?"

In their rush to address problem situations, companies often just pick a solution and announce it rather than getting input. That is appropriate in some cases, but in others, it is a missed opportunity for not only getting input that will help them make the best choice, but also demonstrating their desire to do the very best thing for all involved.

In most cases, a company is dealing with an issue affecting their current products or services, so they are dealing with their customers, not the marketplace at large. They know exactly how to get in touch with them, and they can choose the communications mode that is going to get them to all of their customers as quickly and effectively as possible.

Now, there is a caveat here. In any survey situation, you need to manage people's expectations so that you are very clear from the start what the possible choices are. You may have a scenario wherein theoretically you have three choices for addressing it, but as a practical matter only one that can be implemented.

In that situation, you must take care not to give people choices that you are not certain you would be able or willing to implement if they were to choose them. In this kind of situation, you choose that one workable solution and then consider alternatives for communicating about it.

You may have an opportunity for using a survey to get input on how you are going to implement that choice, when you have more than one workable implementation option.

In other circumstances, you may have several workable alternatives that you are willing to give people as choices, but you can only implement one of them. In that case, you let people know that they have input on the choice, but that only one choice will be implemented.

If all the choices are equally acceptable to the company and the only remaining criteria is what most customers want, then it may be that whatever the majority wants, that is what everyone is going to get.

If that is the case, then that is what you tell people up front. You want to be sure they understand that "voting" for a particular alternative does not guarantee getting it. When you ask them the question, you explain this diplomatically, but very clearly.

Now, somebody would probably ask me at this point, don't you run the danger of making people angry if you give them a choice to vote and then their vote is not the one that gets selected? They may ask, "Can't you do it differently for each of us?"

Carter: Yes. You just took the words right out of my mouth.

Marie: It is a good question. The answer to that is yes, there is some risk and you have to assess that risk on the front end. Decide whether asking for their input gets you more goodwill than the potential bad will from someone who is disappointed when their way does not get selected.

Carter: I recall a situation in which I bought something from a major company that was putting a lot of money behind their marketing to convince people to change to this new thing. However, the product was obviously not that great once you got it and started using it. It left a lot to be desired, and the market was left feeling flat about it. I certainly was.

However, then I received a survey since I had purchased their product. It asked me questions about the product, but it did not give me the means or the mechanism to be able to comment on the things that I felt were problems. In addition, the survey did not seem to acknowledge that there was a problem with the product. This was a real disconnect from reality, especially since the business press and consumer online forums were all talking about all the problems with this product.

The survey questions themselves seemed to be trying to steer away from the obvious problems. Maybe their thought was that they already knew all about those issues, so no need to ask for input. However, in the absence of acknowledgement, it made you wonder if they were just trying to "fake you out." It was sort of like the old joke, you know, "Other than that, Mrs. Lincoln, how did you like the play?" They seemed to gloss over the obvious things and did not give customers the chance to express their own frustrations with the product.

I found myself thinking, you know, if they had just given me an opportunity, I would have felt at least a little better about the situation. Even if they had heard it from a lot of other people and that took care of their need for information, it did not take care of my need to vent.

If they had given me, a user of their product, the opportunity to tell them what it was I did not like about it, it would have made me feel at least that they cared. Instead, I was left wondering if they cared and whether or not they were going to address the real issues that so many people were talking about.

Marie: Carter, that is a great example of what happens when companies are not sensitive enough to what their customers are feeling, as well as the need to give them a mechanism to be heard. Companies really hurt themselves in this situation, because not only are customers unhappy with that particular product, but they also remember their negative feelings about that brand in general and are much less likely to buy from the company again if they have a choice.

Carter: Yes, that is exactly right. As a consumer, I can respect honesty and transparency on their part in acknowledging that not every product is a home run. Most people understand that companies are not always going to "hit one out of the park" every time they "step up to the plate," and that not every product is going to meet every need. However, they do not tolerate being ignored well at all.

In the survey I referred to, it seemed as though the company did not want to acknowledge what was common knowledge in the industry about their latest product. I am hearing you say that companies need to be honest and that the questions in the survey need to reflect the real current situation. It seems that using a survey to get at the real issues and to communicate clearly will benefit both the customers and the company.

In fact, it seems that companies can even come out on the other side having stronger relationships than if they had not bothered to involve their customers in the first place. Am I hearing you right? Are those some of the ideas that you are expressing?

Marie: Yes. That is exactly right, and you touched on something there, Carter, worth remarking on again. There has been a lot of change in people's lives over the last 10 years. The "uncertainty quotient" is a lot higher in peoples' lives because of the scars from 9/11, because so many corporate giants have fallen or been shown to be dishonest and because of economic challenges.

People are even more concerned about making good choices, being safe and being well treated. They want to know that they can trust the companies that they do business with and that those companies care about their well-being, beyond what is in their wallets. People understand that companies are there to make money and there is nothing wrong with that. However, they do not want to feel that they are being taken advantage of.

We have talked about it before, but it bears repeating. More than ever before, people appreciate a company that treats them fairly and routinely demonstrates their good faith. This is a huge competitive advantage. Given a choice between saving some money with one company and doing business with another company that you trust more, many people will pick the trustworthy company. They are going to pick the company that they can trust, because a bargain is not a bargain if the product is not going to work or if you have problems with it, but you cannot get any help.

Companies who get a reputation for being hard to deal with, selfish, uncaring or just ignorant about their customers' needs do not succeed in the long haul. One way to avoid these things is to stay in close touch with your customers, especially when there is a problem.

Research has shown that the most loyal customers are not those who have never had a problem. It is those who have had a problem that the company handled well. They left the customer with a feeling that they were caring, honest and responsive. These people are the most loyal customers.

As we discussed above, in some situations surveys are a way to collectively address issues that are affecting many customers. They can be a vehicle for demonstrating the honesty and caring that matter to people.

Here is something else to consider. I have heard you say that companies do not own their brand anymore, because in this day and age there are so many ways that everyone can communicate with one another, so companies have much less control of what is communicated about their brand. The Internet has leveled the playing field in ways no one imagined ten years ago.

Online reviews are a case in point. The customer comment and product review sections of companies' websites are essentially ongoing surveys. People can post their reviews, and it does not appear that the companies censor them. So far, every one I have ever seen had negative as well as positive comments. Some of them were very negative, like "I wouldn't buy this product." or "You can't get any help from customer service." Forums and sites specializing in online product reviews for specific industries are another example of this. It is a whole new world now that customers have access to information on an unprecedented level.

Smart consumers know in looking at something like this that if 1% or 10% of the people are unhappy and 90% are happy then that is a good sign about the product or the company. On the other hand, if they go in and see a majority of negative feedback, then they take that as a real caution sign or even an absolute "don't buy this on a bet" sign.

These online review sites could be viewed by the company as a survey, and all the keys to doing surveys successfully could be applied in this situation as well. You have the opportunity to make it a two-way conversation, not one that is defensive, but one that is informative.

Carter: Right.

Marie: I look for the pattern in the postings and every time I see significant evidence that the company will not stand behind its product, then I am immediately wary. I do not care how good the company says it is. I do not care how cheap it is. I do not care if, on the face of it, it looks like the exact solution to the thing I am trying to address. If a significant number of people are consistently reporting negatively on the company's product, service or responsiveness, then I do not want to go there! I am unwilling to spend my time beating my head against a brick wall. I would rather find another solution and deal with a company that treats people right. I am far from unique in this regard.

Carter: I think you are right. I am in the same camp. It baffles me that some companies just do not allow a mechanism for any kind of feedback. It baffles me even more that some companies do as you describe and do not use online postings as a way to communicate.

Marie: You may send a survey out because there is a problem with your product or service and you want to involve your customers in addressing it. Alternatively, you can have some kind of ongoing online product review or other site where customers can post comments. Either way, the smart company can use this to build stronger relationships, better products and services and improved brand image.

Key Points Summary

Using Surveys as a Vehicle to
Communicate When There Are Problems

- Surveys can be a vehicle for communication when there is a problem

- Determine if your situation involves a choice that customers could make

- Make the pros and cons of each choice clear

- Manage expectations so that your customers know what they can expect and not expect

- Realize that your company online product review and comment sites function as surveys

- Consider using your online review and comment sites for two-way communication

- Look for predominant patterns of input to use as part of market intelligence gathering

Chapter Eight

Creative Ways to Connect with Your Target Market

"There are more ways than ever before to connect with your customers in this digital age."

Chapter Eight

Creative Ways to Connect with Your Target Market

You must first consider whether your customer is a consumer or another business.

Business-to-Business

If you are in the business-to-business market, then the key here is how you select who gives you the feedback and how you get to that person. You need to get this information from the person spending the money or approving the purchase and from the person with the most information about how your product or service must meet their needs, if that is a different person. If you do not know who this would be with certainty, then contact someone in the company to ask. In fact, this is a great opportunity to establish a closer relationship if you don't already have one by contacting one of those people and asking them the best way to connect with them to get their input.

This is also an opportunity to confirm what position to reach out to if you are sending a survey to another company. In the case of your current customer who is another business, you may know specifically who the person is, or you can easily find out and address them directly.

Business-to-Consumer

If your target market is consumers, this can seem daunting because it can be a very large target market depending on your product. About now, you may be saying to yourself that this all sounds good, but you do not know how to get a survey to your target population.

You know how to reach your current customers, but not how to reach out to your market in general. To help you out, we are going to take a little side trip here into the "nuts and bolts" of surveys.

What are your best options for getting the survey to your target population and the relative advantages and disadvantages of each option for each survey's particular target population?   Do you remember the earlier discussion about knowing clearly who your target audience is? You need to be sure you have gotten that clear first. Then ask yourself:

1. Where are they?

2. What are the practical options for connecting them with your survey?

3. Which of those options is the best one or ones to connect with them?

4. In the case of more than one option, consider testing all the options with a sample from your target market to see if one works significantly better than the others do.

For each survey, consider a variety of sources for connecting with possible respondents. You may need more than one method in order to attract the number of respondents you want in the time frame that you need.

Methods of Recruiting Survey Respondents

There are many ways you can publicize your survey. Here is a list of some of the methods you might consider using:

- Social media, such as Facebook and Twitter

- Email to your own list of customers or prospects

- Letter or postcard to your list

- Letter or postcard to rented opt-in list

- Phone call to your list or rented opt-in list

- Internet articles with link to survey

- Blog containing, or with link to, survey

- Press release (online or off line)

- Notice on your own or others' websites

- Mail or email to joint venture partner's list

- Newsgroup, forum, or listserv postings, if permitted

- Personal network

- Google, Yahoo or other Pay-Per-Click (PPC)

- Print advertisements in magazines or newspapers

- Paid advertisements on others' targeted sites

- Store handouts or notices

- Television advertisements

- Announcements at conventions or meetings

- Bulk coupon mailer

- Inserts in others' targeted mailings

- Notice with link info in product shipment

- Notice with link in purchase thank you emails

- Website exit pop-ups or pop-overs with survey link

We will explore each of these options for connecting with your potential survey respondents. Each one has advantages and disadvantages. If you are clear about the benefits that you expect to receive from doing your survey, then you will be able to weigh the specific advantages and disadvantages of each one of the options in relation to what you are specifically trying to do.

Social Media

One of the fastest growing, most efficient means of connecting today is Social Media. It is also free. For business applications, Facebook and Twitter are considered the best choices. Many companies now have pages, also called fan pages on Facebook.

Recently a leading snack manufacturer launched a new flavor using social media, instead of their own website. More and more companies are developing and actively using a social media presence.

TWTPoll and TWTSurvey, at those .com addresses, allow you to create polls or surveys that you can integrate with the Twitter, Facebook and other social media platforms. It includes multiple question type options, as well as an option to use images rather than text questions. Look into Social Media for your company. It can provide a way to connect with your market on an ongoing basis, as well as a way to advertise your survey or actually do your survey.

Email to Your Own List

E-mailing to your own lists is one of the most obvious choices in contacting potential respondents for your survey. The obvious advantage of this is that you already have these people available to you. If they are your current customers or prospects that you have been communicating with regularly, then they are more likely than total strangers would be to respond to a survey for you.

Conversely, the most obvious disadvantage is that these will be people whom you already have available on your list; therefore, you will not be able to use the survey process for reaching out to someone new.

Letter or Postcard to Your List

Sending a letter or a postcard to your list has the same advantages and disadvantages as e-mailing to your own list does. If you choose this option, it is important to make your invitation brief and clear. You must ensure that the instruction for taking the survey is readily apparent to the potential respondent when they open the mailing or first view a postcard, and that it is something appealing.

This applies whether it is a paper survey included with the mailing or an online survey wherein you are sending the respondent to a particular web page via an included link.

Some marketers have had success with sending a series of postcards inviting participation in the survey. In this case, the survey is online, and the postcard simply gets the recipient curious enough or motivated enough to go to the website and check things out further.

Letter or Postcard to Rented Opt-In List

The advantages and disadvantages of sending to a rented opt-in list are similar to those outlined above, whether an e-mail list or a physical mailing list. Opt-in means that a person asked to be on the list. In a double opt-in list, the person also confirmed their request. Great care must be taken in choosing a list. Confirm that the list is an opt-in list. Find out if it is single or double opt-in. Response rates can be better on a double opt-in list. Many purchased or rented lists are not opt-in. This can lay you open to charges of spamming, and response rates will not be as good.

You must evaluate the quality of the list as to how fresh and accurate the data is, as well as how much care has been taken in the opt-in process, if it claims to be an opt-in list. You must also evaluate the potential returns based on the quality of the list, the cost of renting the list and other costs in relation to potential ROI.

You may also consider a rented list that is not opt-in. In that event, you may normally expect a lower response rate unless what you are surveying about is very compelling in some way and of particular interest to the list that you have rented. There is the concern about spamming. Cold lists like this tend to produce lower response rates, because you have no relationship with the people.

Phone Call to Your List or Rented Opt-In List

Phone calls to a rented opt-in list have similar advantages and disadvantages as outlined above. In addition, because of resistance to telemarketers, you may find it more difficult to get people to agree to take the survey even when you simply wish to direct them to a website, as opposed to requesting that they take the survey on the spot.

Unfortunately, in this instance, follow through is not likely to be good unless you have offered a desirable incentive that they can only obtain by taking the survey. As outlined in Chapter Five, there are also pros and cons of actually doing surveys over the telephone.

Internet Articles with Link to Survey

Internet articles with a link to your survey can be a very good strategy for connecting with your target market if they typically browse online for articles on your topic. If you do not know if your target market does this, but you strongly suspect that they do, one way to find out is to do a mini survey and ask if they use article directories or search for articles on line. Of course, to do this you still have to get a list to send to or drive traffic to a website where the survey is located.

Blog Containing, or with Link to, Survey

The question, when considering links on a blog as a potential way to reach your respondents, is how well you are driving traffic to your blog and what your specific traffic volume is in relation to how quickly you need to find sufficient respondents for your survey.

If you have a well-trafficked blog, this can be a very effective approach. You might also consider linking this approach with one of the other online approaches designed to drive traffic to your blog. People will get the survey link and simultaneously be introduced to your blog.

Press Release - Online or Offline

Press releases as a way of driving traffic to a survey have been successful for some marketers. The key here is in doing an effective press release through channels that will get you a lot of exposure. One of the most popular press release engines on the Internet with an excellent track record for exposure is PRweb.com.

As an interesting twist on this, marketers have also used press releases about survey results to generate interest in their product or service and drive traffic to their website.

Notice on Your Own or Others' Websites

Posting a notice on your website or websites of others who are not competitive with your product or service, but do share the same target market can be very effective. This depends a great deal on how much traffic the websites are getting. It is generally not recommended to just wholesale post links to your survey wherever you can get them, because you are not targeting the population you are specifically interested in, in that case.

Online links and ads on your current website are another way to post notices. You can add links to your existing website that showcase your product or service, and then ask users if they would be interested in joining an ongoing online advisory panel. The primary target here, obviously, is your current customers or users who are already interested in your product or service. You can offer incentives for participating, such as special reports or "privileged status" discounts on new products and the like.

Mail or Email to Joint Venture Partner List

Joint venture partner in this context does not mean a legal partner. Rather, it means someone with whom you have an arrangement such that they will be getting something in return for helping you, or who has some other motivation for allowing you to access their list.

Usually the connection, other than friendship, is that the product you are researching is one that their list may be likely to buy.

Therefore, they are willing to help you with your survey because of later potential benefits when your new or updated product is ready. Through a joint venture setup, they receive a commission on each sale of your product or service made to people they referred. There may also be reciprocal situations wherein you send surveys to your respective lists for each other.

Sending to a joint venture partner's list is one of the most effective approaches to getting respondents for your survey. In this scenario, your joint venture partner directly encourages the people on his or her list to take your survey. Since they already have a relationship with their own list, they have more credibility than a stranger does. Generally, you will also need to offer something of value such as a free report to encourage people to participate.

The same guidelines apply as in other situations in which you are accessing someone else's customer base, that is, it is critical to get with partners who share the same target market as yours. In the online community in particular, joint ventures for introducing products are very popular, and a survey to a joint venture partner's list could well be done as the first step in a process that culminates in a product launch.

Newsgroup, Forum or Listserv Postings, if Permitted

Newsgroups, forums, and listservs can be an effective place to post a link to your survey if that is permitted by the group and if you choose the group carefully in relation to how well it matches your target market.

Personal Network

Do not forget about your personal network. Family, friends, colleagues and acquaintances can be good sources for getting survey respondents, depending upon the nature of your survey. If your survey is on an issue likely to be of interest to the broader public, then people you know socially may be able to spread the word effectively for you, particularly if they themselves have extensive mailing lists.

Google, Yahoo, or Other Pay-Per-Click (PPC)

This approach is definitely not recommended as a do-it-yourself project if you are not already experienced with it. It can be very costly and not very productive if you do not know exactly what you are doing. If you are not experienced and you want to do this, you are best off hiring a professional in this area to do it for you.

Google or Yahoo pay-per-click (or any pay-per-click program) is one choice for driving traffic to a website for a survey link. This approach can work not only for the primary purpose of getting respondents for your survey, but it can also be effective in the early stages of a product introduction wherein you want to test your online sales letter and you require significant traffic in a short period of time early in your campaign.

You can advertise your survey, offer a gift for participating in the survey, take them directly to your survey and then at the end of the survey offer a link to your regular website with your product or service information.

Alternatively, you can take them directly to your website and offer the survey link in a prominent place there. Even if they choose not to participate in the survey, you got them to your website. If you choose this approach, take care that you are not doing it in such a way that will be perceived as bait and switch by those who clicked on your survey advertisement. Make sure that your advertisement is worded in such a way that it is both appealing and not misleading.

Print Advertisements in Magazines or Newspapers

Print ads will only work well in driving traffic to your survey, usually on a website, if the topic of your survey is a good match for the readers of that publication. Obviously the better targeted the publication is to your market and your product or service, the better response rate and quality respondents you'll get and the more potential benefit you can receive.

However, in some cases, the best quality match is also going to be an expensive one. This can be especially true if your product is in a large and highly competitive market. It may take a little digging to see if you can unearth an undiscovered jewel that is relatively inexpensive, but still an excellent match for your target market.

This might be a little known publication with lower advertising rates whose readers are a good match for your target population or a subset of your target population for whom specialty publications exist.

Paid Advertisements on Others' Targeted Sites

Advertisements on websites that attract your specific target market can work well depending upon how good the match is to your market and how much benefit you can expect to receive in relation to the cost of the ads. This includes considering both the quality and quantity of the traffic that the site gets, as well as consistency.

Here is a specific example. Targeted advertising on industry specific sites can work. If you are interested in a particular niche industry, this could be a very cost-effective way to go. For example, if you were trying to recruit survey respondents about timeshare interest and issues, you might target advertising on vacation rental sites and timeshare specific related sites.

Store Handouts or Notices

Notices posted in your store or flyers placed in the bag with the customers' purchases may work in some situations, but many people ignore these and toss the flyers. You would almost certainly have to offer an incentive to get people to take the survey. If you have a physical business location, you are likely to be more successful by going the computer kiosk route on site.

Television Advertisements

Television ads might be effective depending upon your target market and their television viewing habits. This is another case in which the notice about the survey and the opportunity to take the survey are separated. It is very likely that you would need to offer an incentive to motivate the viewers to take the survey. Since you reached this population on television, you most likely will want to direct them to a website in order to take the survey.

If your target market and your budget will support a live telephone poll done much the same way as you see on the popular TV shows wherein viewers vote for the best performer, then you would likely get a much higher response rate. However, for many businesses, this may not be a fit due to target market issues or budget issues.

Announcements at Conventions or Meetings

Announcements at meetings have similar disadvantages to any of the other approaches above wherein the survey announcement is separate from the actual opportunity to take the survey. On the other hand, meetings may be pre-sorted for a target market and may be more likely to be composed of individuals with some motivation to take a survey because of their affiliation with that particular group. Each opportunity has to be evaluated separately.

Bulk Coupon Mailers

Mailers offering a gift for taking the survey also suffer from the same disadvantages as any of the other approaches in which the announcement about the survey is separate from the opportunity to take the survey. You would have to evaluate if there are advantages to this approach for your particular target market.

Inserts in Others' Targeted Mailings

This approach has the advantage of being more targeted and of possibly gaining credibility through association, depending upon whose mailing you are in. It has the same disadvantages as the other approaches wherein the opportunity to take the survey is not immediate, in the sense that it requires more action and initiative from people than it would if they could simply click on a link or fill out the form right that minute without having to go anywhere else to do it.

Paper Notice with Link Info in Your Product Shipment

This approach may appear to have the same disadvantages as those outlined above. However, because the insert is in your product shipment that means that you already have a relationship with that person because he or she is already your customer. Your odds of getting a response in this situation are better than if you are dealing with total strangers who have no relationship with your company.

Notice with Link in Purchase Thank You Emails

This approach is similar to the one just above except that the notice is sent via e-mail instead of being a flyer in a physical shipment. Obviously, this approach would make sense if you were selling digital download products. It also has the advantage of allowing the person to immediately click on the link and take the survey right away. This tends to improve your response rate.

Website Exit Pop-Ups or Pop-Overs with Survey Link

Website exit pop-ups or pop-overs have become popular enough online that some people are tired of them. A major factor here is having a software script for this that is not annoying. Many marketers have had success with simple pop-ups containing a single question and often a verbal cue to stop and read the pop-up.

You may have experienced these when you attempt to exit a site and a pop-up shows up with a voiceover asking you to "Stop!" or "Don't leave yet!" or "Before you leave would you help us out by ..." or something similar followed by a short explanation of the request to answer just one question or take some other action.

Other Observations

If your survey is web based, then it is easy to use many different modes of recruitment to drive potential participants to the website. If, in your judgment, it will not deter too many people from taking the survey, then consider setting it up so that you collect their email address on the front end before you send them to the survey. The reason you give for this is so that you can send them the link to the downloadable gift you are giving them for taking the survey. Of course, then you do have to be offering a gift.

Criteria to Consider in Evaluating
Respondent Recruitment Options

- Time required
- Money required in relation to budget and ROI
- Fit with the respondent population you want to attract
- Ease or difficulty of implementation
- Manpower required
- Opportunity to and importance of building on this method for future surveys

Return to the beginning of this chapter to see the summary list of all the survey distribution options that were explored here.

Chapter Nine

Steps to Skyrocketing Your Sales and Profits with a Strategic Market Survey System

"In-depth market intelligence coupled with a strong target market relationship equals competitive advantage that drives superior sales and profits."

Chapter Nine

Steps to Skyrocketing Your Sales and Profits with a Strategic Market Survey System

In this chapter, we will examine one way to approach implementing a survey-based strategy for your company. These steps are listed in the order in which you should do them.

1. Determine who in your company should be involved in the discussion about your use of a survey strategy to gather market intelligence and build relationships with your current customers and market.

2. Take my free proprietary **Market IQ** assessment, which you can access by going to the link provided below. This will help you enormously in focusing your efforts in building a stronger relationship with your market and your current customers.

    Have the person or persons most familiar with your strategies and practices in market research, as well as maintaining contact with your customers, do the Market IQ assessment. You can access it here:

    www.MarketSurveyMastery.com/BookOwnerMarketIQ.php

3. Review the Key Points Summary for each chapter in this book. Make a list of what you plan to try for your company.

4. Set up a meeting with the people you identified in step one to be included in discussing the survey-based strategy and its

applications for your company. Provide an overview of this strategy based on the Key Points Summary from Chapter Two in this book and your notes from step three above.

Hand out copies of the Market IQ assessment completed by assigned person per step number 2. Review the results of the Market IQ assessment. Do not consider the answers given by the assigned person to be final. You may find some surprising points of view about the issues covered in the Market IQ as you discuss and review the questions.

5. Make a decision as to whether or not your company is going to pursue this survey strategy. Remember, the objectives are to gather market intelligence, build relationships to increase sales and profits and build competitive advantage.

    Consider your other strategies for addressing these three objectives, how effective they are and what they require in resources. Compare current or projected ROI from each strategy to help you make this decision.

6. Based on having completed the steps above and considering what your business goals and situation are, decide which kind of survey you should do first and why. The most common reasons for doing market or customer surveys are:

    - Get input from current customers on your products and services

    - Get input from current customers on your customer service

    - Get input from visitors to your web site about the site

- General market research to get a feel for the wants and needs in your market

- Get input from current customers and target market on new products or services you are considering

7. Create a Survey Project Action Plan specifying each step in the process, including timelines.   Many businesses underestimate the time required to complete tasks.   Be realistic in your planning.   You should plan for your data analysis when you are planning your project.   Have we identified specific time in our schedule for analyzing the data when it comes in?   Do we have plans for involving others in the company in the data analysis?

This is important, not only for "mining the gold" in the data effectively, but also for making decisions about the right follow up action to take and having the people who will be in charge of implementation fully informed and on board.

Plan ample time in your schedule to be able to do a thorough analysis of the data once it is compiled, usually by using software.   Involve others as appropriate in this.   Allow additional time for analyzing open-ended question responses as these will take longer than numerical summaries to analyze.

Then strategize and make follow up plans both for communicating with your survey respondents and implementing the actions that you have decided to take.

This is where the payoff in doing surveys really comes, so do not skimp on the time to do this right, and do not wait to do it until the data is old and no longer valid.

8. Create your survey questions and test them.

9. Distribute your survey.

10. Analyze the data to determine trends and patterns as well as new information

11. Decide what action to take in response to survey results

12. Communicate your plans inside and outside the company, as appropriate, especially to the people who responded to your survey.

13. Implement your plan and then evaluate its impact.

14. Repeat the process, each survey building on the one before, so that you create a dialogue with your target market and/or your current customers.

Here is a little reminder as to why you want to do this.

- You obtain accurate market intelligence that you can act on profitably

- You develop strong ongoing relationships with your market and current customers

- You create competitive advantage that supports top notch sales and profits performance, now and in the future

Chapter Ten

Tips on How to Be
Most Successful
with Strategic Market Surveys

*"You will have the edge over your competition
in applying this strategy to create
success for your business."*

Chapter Ten

Tips on How to Be Most Successful
with Strategic Market Surveys

There are some common mistakes that companies make in using surveys. All of them are easy to avoid if you know them in advance. Many of them have been mentioned in other chapters. This is your summary checklist for **what not to do** when you implement this strategic survey strategy.

A. **Failure to clearly specify the objectives in doing your survey**

The key here is to understand that you must be crystal clear up front about why you are doing the survey. Before you ever start to write survey questions, answer the following questions and write down your answers. This is important because it provides the context for everything else you do in this process.

1. What is the ultimate business objective that will be served by this survey process?
2. What is it that you are trying to understand or get more information about?
3. What do you intend to do with what you discover?

B. **Failure to precisely identify your survey's target population**

While it may seem obvious, you must clearly define, in writing, to whom the survey is directed. This also provides context and directly impacts what questions you choose and how you write them.

Specify all relevant demographics. Examples include such variables as gender, age, race, location, income, current customer (or not), owner of a specific product (or not) and so forth.

C. **Failure to carry the survey process all the way through so as to reap the benefits**

You avoid this pitfall by creating a complete project plan at the beginning. In it, you lay out all the phases and steps of the process along with a schedule of activities and a list of resources required. Include everything from survey design to the follow up steps and everything in between such as data analysis.

This is especially important for larger survey projects involving many departments in your organization or for multiple survey projects with a single objective, such as what you might do when gathering information for new product or service design.

D. **Addressing more than one subject in a single question**

This one sounds simple, but is surprisingly easy to mess up. Read your questions carefully. If you ask, what they think about two different things, then it is likely that you have two questions embedded in one. One quick way to tell this is that any time that you have a survey question with the word "and" in it, check to see what comes before and after the "and." Even if they are related to each other, if it is possible for a person to answer the two parts in different ways or if they really are separate issues, then you need to make them separate questions. Otherwise, when you look at your data, you will not know what the survey takers were responding to when they answered. This kind of situation is also frustrating for your survey respondents.

E. **Writing questions that are too long or that contain unfamiliar jargon or hard to understand vocabulary**

The longer the question, the more likely it is that readers will get confused, tired, or bored. Then they are likely to bail on the question or even the whole survey process.

Avoid jargon, unless it is pertinent to your target population. Avoid using big words when more common, easy to understand ones will do. The reading level should match your audience. For general situations, eighth grade is a good approximation.

F. **Expectations about what the data will say that result in biased question creation**

This is a case of "garbage in – garbage out." It is very easy for a bias to sneak into your questions, either because of what you already believe the answers will be or because of what you want them to be. Review the way your questions are written carefully to ensure that you have in no way suggested what the answer should be.

G. **Not using a combination of narrative response (open-ended) and multiple or single choice (closed-ended) questions**

Narrative responses give you more information, because you have not limited what the respondents can tell you. They do, however, take longer to do and will wear out your respondents more quickly. Multiple or single choice responses take less time and allow you to do statistical analysis of the responses, but the information you get is limited precisely by the response choices presented with the question asked. Adding an "Other" choice will help with this.

H. **Making your survey too long**

This discourages people from participating and increases the probability of confusion or fatigue or premature exit from your survey. Groups that you already have a relationship with are more likely to take the time to answer a longer survey.

Telling them up front how much time the survey will take is helpful. Something along the lines of "Please take this short survey. It will only take you Z minutes." How do you know what Z is? The answer to that is you test your survey in advance with a small group. See the next item.

I. **Failure to test your survey for time and clarity with a small pilot group before distributing broadly**

Arrange to have a small group of people, 10 are sufficient, to take your survey and then immediately give you feedback on clarity and flow of the questions. Ask half a dozen questions about their experience of the survey, so you are doing a "survey on your survey." That is how you find out if your questions were as clear as you thought they were.

Often, there will be something that made sense to you, but does not make sense to other people. You find this out and correct it before you send it out to the larger population. Then you get quality data.

You also want to ask your survey pilot group to make note of how long it takes them to complete the survey. Gather that information, along with their other comments on the survey experience, so that you know how long the survey takes. If that time turns out to be longer than your target population is likely to be willing to take, then seriously consider shortening your survey.

J. **Using too small a sample size to get an accurate representation of your target market**

If your target market or customer base is very large, for most surveys, assuming that your recruitment process results in a representative sample of your market, a sample of about 400 will suffice regardless of how large your target market is. It is critical to address getting a representative sample of your market. It is generally useful to use a variety of strategies to recruit participants to address both of these issues.

If your customer base is very small, for example under 100 people, you will obviously be dealing with a smaller number for a sample, but that number will be a greater percent of the whole. For example, with a total population of only 40, you would need to get 36 responses to be reasonably sure of your data. You do not have to understand the mathematics of probability and sampling to determine how many people you need to answer your survey for you to be confident that the data is representative. Just go online and search the term "sample size calculators," and you will find plenty of options. Many of them are free.

K. **Failure to address data use and privacy issues in your survey invitation**

People are more likely to agree to participate if they know how you are going to use the data and, if you collect personal information, they must be assured that their privacy will be protected. It is simple enough to address this at the beginning of each survey that you do.

Do remember the difference between "confidential" and "anonymous." Confidential means that you will know who said what, but you will not disclose that to anyone.

"Anonymous" means that no one knows who made which answers.

Written and online surveys are often done anonymously to encourage more people to respond. If you are doing a confidential survey wherein you know who answered each survey, or you are doing interviews, always assure people that their particular answers will not be associated with their names and that their names will not be shared outside the company. Take steps to ensure that this is so.

L. **Not combining data collection methodologies for the best coverage, for example, written questionnaires going to large numbers of people and interviews with a small number of people.**

Conducting both written and interview surveys is usually a very powerful and effective approach. In interviews, you have two-way communication and can ask clarification and follow-up questions. Typically, you should do a small number of interviews first, because what you find out there will help you to create better questions for your written survey, including, but not limited to determining the most important issues for you to ask about. Interviews are also effective as follow up to a written survey when you want to explore a particular issue in more depth.

M. **Failure to follow through with timely action and communication to your survey respondents, based on what you discover from the survey**

This is one of the most common mistakes people make in using surveys. When you ask people to take their time and share their thoughts or feelings with you, you create an entirely reasonable expectation on their part that you will do something useful with what they gave you.

It is a psychological contract. To fulfill your end of this implied contract and reap benefits from conducting a survey, you must analyze the data you collect, determine what action you should take based on what you discover, and take that action in a timely way. Then be sure to let your respondents know that you not only greatly appreciate their input, but also that you are definitely doing something meaningful with it.

N. **Not leveraging the connections you make**

You are not only asking questions, you are also building relationships. Think in terms of an ongoing process of engaging your customers and prospects with you in an ongoing survey process, rather than as a single event. If you do this well, they will come to know you, like you and trust you and consequently will prefer to do business with you instead of competitors with whom they do not have that kind of relationship.

O. **Not setting up a system for ongoing survey use in your company, focused on both gathering market intelligence and building stronger relationships with your current customers and target market**

A simple system arranged so that you are automatically cued to continue in an ongoing survey process is a good beginning. Without some structure, it is easy to let survey completion, action and an ongoing survey process fall prey to the other demands on the company's resources.

Chapter Eleven

Multiply the Impact of Strategic Market Surveys for Greater Business Results

*"The reward in booming sales and profits
now and in the future, as well as
a compelling competitive advantage,
is more than worth the effort."*

Chapter Eleven

Multiply the Impact of Strategic Market Surveys for Greater Business Results

Check your survey process to ensure that you address all of these points and apply them to your situation appropriately. Some of these have been covered elsewhere in this book. Others are the reverse of what not to do, with some additional insights on what to do. Still others are new information. Together, they constitute a convenient summary of steps to take to ensure maximum benefit from engaging in an ongoing strategic survey process for your company.

A. **Always see survey use in gathering market intelligence as an ongoing process,** not an event. Make your plans accordingly, so that survey content builds upon previous survey discoveries and enables you to get continually clearer on what your marketplace wants, needs, desires and fears or yearns to solve.

B. **Involve others in the company** who are directly involved in the sales, marketing and product design of your company's product in the design of your survey. Not only will your surveys be better, but the structure provided by the survey discussion will result in:

- Better teamwork

- More clarity across the company about what you are doing or planning on doing

- More opportunity for intelligent input by those same people when it comes time to analyze your survey data

- More commitment to the end results of the survey when it comes time to make decisions and take action on what you discovered.

C. **Use surveys as a prime opportunity to build relationships and good will with your prospects and customers:**

- Engage them actively in an ongoing process wherein you ask questions and share information

- Hear what they tell you

- Discover what that means

- Decide what you should do about it

- Communicate your plans and excitement

- Take action

- Communicate about the action

- Ask more questions in an ongoing cycle.

D. **Throughout the process, build more good will** by being generous with your gifts and your thanks. Make it clear that you value them and their input. It will come back to you many times over.

Plan, in advance, and then review once the survey is done, how you will stay in touch with the survey participants. Consider what other helpful and generous things you can do for them. This is in addition to, and after, your original thank you or any inducement to take the survey, if there was one.

E. **Always follow through on your survey process** once you have the data and ensure that you:

- Analyze the data promptly

- Decide what the implications of the data are for your business and what the best, most timely action is for you to take

- Make a plan for that action and implement it

- Evaluate the impact of that action

- Communicate what will be most helpful and interesting for others. Communicate not only to customers and to prospects as indicated above, but within your own company as well. Ask yourself, "Who would benefit from knowing this, and how will it benefit both them and our company?"

F. **Implement your follow-up communications plan diligently**, the one you made after you did your data analysis, determined what actions you were going to take, what to communicate and to whom. Here are some additional things to consider in your follow-up plan.

- **Customized Subgroup Follow up:**

   If your survey software or other survey procedure allowed you to track emails or other contact information in such a way that you can associate them with data subsets created in your analysis, then you have an opportunity to customize your follow up. You can then tailor your communication and further surveys based specifically on the information you gleaned in your analysis.

   In doing this, you are categorizing people that feel the same way about answering a question. You can send out specific follow-ups to those people to ask them more or to start leading them to the next step in a buying process or, perhaps, you will ask them to refer people to you who have similar interests.

Whatever the desired outcome is, you now have information categorized in such a way that you can use it more effectively. You can better communicate with groups of people who feel the same about a particular question or group of questions.

- **Follow-up Interviews**

  Although a written survey can gather information from a large number of people about a wide range of subjects, it does not provide the in-depth information that a face-to-face interview provides.

  Because of this, many organizations conduct personal follow-up interviews with as much as 20% to 30% of the original survey sample. Even a small sample on the order of 5% to 10% can provide much enlightenment.

  Select this smaller group carefully. Take special care to make certain that this subgroup is a truly representative sample of those in the survey.

  How do you decide what to ask in the follow-up interview? The following steps will help you identify areas that could profit from additional probing.

  - o Examine open-ended questions and "write-in" comments. These indicate what respondents feel strongly about. They usually will welcome an opportunity to talk more about them.

o   Check areas wherein the responses are not
clear or where the conclusions are vague.
Follow up interviews or surveys can greatly
help in further clarifying these areas.

o   Look for results that surprised you. These
areas also provide interesting and profitable
points for further analysis.

G.   **Ongoing Communication**

Remember, ongoing communication is the key. You can
find many reasons to be in touch with your prospects and
customers if you stay focused on the "AHA" experience.
Ask + Hear + Act = The AHA experience

It is critical to determine what you will communicate to the
respondents after the survey:

- Share key findings and insights of interest to them

- Let them know what you plan to do

- Invite them to stay involved

- Give heartfelt thanks again

- Actually do what you say you will

- Make an action plan

- Evaluate results and revise as needed

- Share interesting or exciting announcements with
your participants

- Ask for more input via a survey when you need it

- Continue the cycle of Ask, Hear, and Act (AHA!)

H. **Use the survey process to build relationships with "thought leaders"** and other influential persons in your industry by getting them involved in your process. Do this by asking to interview them as part of your survey process. You can:

- Ask their opinion on what the greatest challenges or trends in your industry are

- Ask for input on what they feel are the most important questions to ask of your market at this point in time (which you would, of course, take as input only to consider with all the other factors in your survey)

- Ask permission to record the interview for your own notes

- Ask if you may share a copy of it and/or a transcript of it with the people who take your survey, visit your website, or are your customers and whatever else that you would like to use it for.

This is a great way to get some quality input from a recognized authority, or a person with great credentials who may not be well known, but who will have credibility when you share their credentials. Stress that you will not be charging for sharing the information and that he or she will receive full credit for their contribution.

If they agree, be sure to compose your interview questions in advance and send those to them for review, input and approval so that they are comfortable and ready when you interview them. You can do this in person or on the phone. You can find these authorities through industry publications, in your local area, and at universities. If you handle it the right way, you will get experts who will do this for you.

Of course, you offer them a copy of the recording and the transcript along with your thanks.

Ask if they would like to know what happens with the survey. For those that are interested, you may be able to build a relationship and come back to them in the future for more interviews, advice, connections, etc.

I. **Create a System for Regular Survey Use In Your Business**

Develop a Simple, Manageable System

1. Set up a routine, for example, at the beginning of the year, generate a list (in concert with your staff or management team, preferably) of areas or issues or questions on which you want to get input from your customers and prospects.

2. Choose one item or issue to focus on and make a commitment to doing the survey process.

3. Set accountability and reminders so that the process does not "slip through the cracks" in the face of other demands on your resources. A simple note on your calendar to check on things at certain intervals can be a big help.

4. Be reasonable, and do not take on more than you can handle.

J. **Build on What You Learn**

1. Have regular conversations focused on what you have learned in your survey process. Make sure that you document what you learn in a way that supports you in using the information effectively.

2. Periodically evaluate how well your system is keeping you on the "survey track." Make adjustments accordingly.

K. Focus On Relationship Building At Least As Much As On Data Gathering

There is not anything complicated to say about this. This is a state of mind to cultivate in order to leverage your survey process fully.

L. Get Creative in Ways to Involve People

1. Brainstorm more ways to get involved with your prospects and customers. Consider a short survey asking them for ideas on how to involve them. Be sure to find out how interested they are in being more involved. Segment your data and associated email addresses or other contact information so that you can follow up specifically with those who indicated an interest in more involvement.

2. Do the same thing with your staff or management team. The issues that you are need to survey about are usually the same ones that your team needs to be informed about, in almost all cases. You want their input related to the meaning of the survey results and their commitment related to the actions to take in response to your conclusions.

3. Consider ways to involve your vendors. Certainly, you can survey them if there are questions you have for them. There are likely to be additional ways to get them involved in the survey process. Some of them may be affected by the actions you choose to

take in response to your survey analysis. Getting them involved earlier in the process can be very helpful to your company and theirs.

It is not "rocket science" to implement this survey strategy. It does require commitment, discipline and, like anything else, action. The rewards in booming sales and profits now and in the future, as well as a compelling competitive advantage, are more than worth the effort.

Chapter Twelve

Ways to Start Benefiting from Strategic Market Surveys Now

*"You don't have to wait to begin
reaping the rewards from this strategy.
The time to do it is now!"*

Chapter Twelve
Ways to Start Benefiting from
Strategic Market Surveys Now

Here are some ways that you can get into this survey strategy right away. See which one makes sense for your business.

A. Interview your current customers

1. Pick a random sample of your current customers. Calculate how many customers you need to survey by going to the Internet and searching for "sample size calculator." Pick one of the free ones that appeals to you and plug in the total number of your current customer base to see how many people you need for a good sample. If it asks for confidence levels and intervals, pick 95% and 5 respectively.

2. Prepare an interview record sheet with name of customer and phone number and name of interviewer at the top. List the questions, leaving room to take notes on what they say.

3. Depending on how many people you want to talk to, divide the calls to be made and assign groups of calls to people in your company who have good interpersonal skills. They do not all have to be in the marketing or customer service departments. In fact, this is good exposure for those who do not normally get to talk to customers.

4. Here are sample questions you can use, or create your own based on an issue you are currently concerned about or interested in.

What do you like most about our product? (If you have more than one product, you must first ask them which they own. Better yet, have that information already on your interview notes sheet, based on the company customer records.)

What do you like least about our product and why?

If there was just one thing you could change about our product, what would it be and why? If this seems like too much, then just pick one question to ask.

5. Collect all the interview notes and review them. Determine what the major themes are and create a list of category names for those themes. Go through the input and assign each one to a category. Count the number of distinct items in each category, as well as how many "hits" each recurring item gets. This will take some time, but what you learn is powerful.

6. Review your summary of what you discovered and discuss what your next step should be. Take it from there.

B. Gather the same data as in number 1 above, but do it in written form.

1. If your customers have computers, decide the best way to get the link for an online survey to them. *See Chapter Eight for help on this.*

2. If you do not already use an online survey service, there are many from which to choose. Survey Monkey is one of my favorites. It has plenty of functionality, a responsive customer service team and very reasonable pricing.

3. Send the link to the survey out to your customers and ask them to respond within a certain period of time. Remember the earlier discussions in this book about how you position the survey by asking them for help and assuring them that they will hear back from you as to what you discover. Address whether the survey is anonymous or confidential.

4. The remainder of the steps is the same as listed in item one above.

C. Surveying your current customers is generally easier than your broader target market because you know how to reach them and they already have a relationship with you, so are more likely to do a survey. Consider a combination of items A and B above. You can do your written survey first. After you analyze the data, decide what you want to know more about. Then implement item A by focusing on the issue you want to explore further. Alternatively, implement A first with a small group of customers to get an idea of what questions and response choices to include on a written survey and then proceed as outlined in item B above.

D. Check out the two surveys I am giving you. (See the Afterword at the end of the book.) If one of them is a good fit for what you would like to know now, first customize the questions to your particular situation as needed. Then proceed as outlined in item two above.

Here is a word of caution. As discussed previously, do not get into surveying about details of features in a proposed product until you have determined the roots of the problem your product would be designed to address. *See Chapter One for a refresher on this as needed.*

E.   Alternatively, you can first carry out the steps outlined in Chapter Nine and then decide which one of the suggestions above makes the most sense for you.

F.   Check out the already prepared surveys in an online survey service of your choice to see whether one of them is a good fit for what you want to explore now. *Doing the steps in Chapter Nine is advised so that you have some criteria for choosing among available surveys.*

Be creative.   Remember that you want to build a relationship, not just gather data. Be sure to follow through in your communication back to your participants. Have some fun with this so your customers have fun, too. They will be more likely to want to play next time.

To get more help on how you can start using this strategy, as well as some special gifts, see the Afterword at the end of this book.

Chapter Thirteen

Executive Summary

"The keys to supercharging your sales and profits and building a strong foundation for the future"

Chapter Thirteen
Executive Summary

Here is a recap of the main points in this book. These are the keys to strategically using market surveys to create stellar business results.

A. Most companies are leaving money on the table, either never earned or wasted, because they do not know their target market and current customers well enough. Assumptions cost your company money every day.

B. People do business with companies that they know, like and trust. They do business with companies that provide the product or service that best meets their specific wants and needs and allays their fears. They do business with the company that solves their problems, fulfills their desires and gives them the best value for their dollar.

C. People make buying decisions emotionally and justify those decisions rationally. You need to know enough to appeal to both aspects of this process.

D. Build enduring relationships with your customers, current and prospective, instead of simply making transactions. The key is to engage your target market and explore their needs, wants, desires, fears, issues and opinions.

E. You must know your customers intimately, even better than they sometimes know themselves, to build superior competitive advantage. Surface exploration with your customers, current and prospective, is not sufficient.

F. Always dig down to your customers' core feelings before embarking on significant changes in any part of your business, including product or service design and customer service strategy. Customers may not even be fully aware of some of their thoughts and feelings. Getting to this core is what sets you apart from the competition and allows you to tailor your products and services to precisely what your customers need and want.

G. Customers' needs and wants are often not the same. You must understand both and offer a solution to them that addresses both or you will not have a satisfied customer. Meeting their wants and allaying their fears provides the motivation for them to buy. Meeting their needs ensures that once they have your product or service, it meets all their expectations – it is a full solution.

H. You cannot bypass buying resistance if you cannot offer value greater than the price of your product or service. You cannot offer that value if you do not know your customer extremely well.

I. You leverage market surveys by simultaneously gathering in-depth market intelligence and using the survey process to build relationships with current and prospective customers.

J. Survey in this context is defined as asking questions, listening carefully to the answers, taking action on those answers and communicating about it to your current customers and target market. The communication is an ongoing conversation, not a one-shot event.

K. More than ever before, customers want to know that companies are honest and genuinely care about their customers. A survey system can significantly support this by not only increasing your understanding of your customer, but also providing an ongoing opportunity to reach out and touch them on a regular basis.

L. A strategic survey system means a system wherein surveys build on one another. When implemented in this way, they provide a platform for both gathering and sharing information, while building relationships.

M. The system is integrated with your strategic direction, which provides the context for what you explore and with whom you explore it, as well as determining the priority of what to explore.

N. A major advantage of the survey strategy is that when consciously focused to do so, it will support improvements in all three of the factors that drive sales: prospect flow, sales conversion and dollar value per customer.

O. Your survey system is invaluable in a product or service development and launch scenario. It not only allows you to get the input you need for product development, but also creates a group of hungry buyers from the people who participated in your ongoing surveys during this process.

P. Technology available today makes doing surveys vastly easier than it once was. There are also many ways to reach your target market to involve them in a survey process, including the many virtual options available today. Social media in particular is already a significant force in business communication and becoming a stronger one all the time. It provides endless opportunities to connect.

Q. People will do surveys if you position them well, manage their expectations on the front end, deliver the survey opportunity conveniently and follow up with them on the results you get and the actions you plan to take. It is a process.

R. Companies of any size can use this strategy. Whether you are 2 or 2000 people strong, you can scale the survey system to meet your particular needs and resources.

S. When trouble strikes, in some situations surveys can be a helpful problem solving and communication tool.

T. Surveys can be a dialogue, a conversation that you carry on mostly virtually with your current customer or target market. When surveys are a real dialogue, you create numerous opportunities to leverage the survey process to your company's benefit.

U. See opportunities for surveying your current customers and target market everywhere! Survey simply means to investigate. It can be one question at a time.

V. The potential ROI on a strategic market survey system is substantial. You will not know what it can do for your company until you try it. If you are already using surveys, revisit them to see how you can further leverage that effort as indicated in this book. If you are not using surveys, there is no time like the present to get started!

Visit the Afterword, just a few pages further on, for some gifts to help you with surveys!

About the Author

Marie Kane has been an entrepreneur, strategic business consultant and executive coach since 1981, following her career as an executive level manager. Her areas of consulting expertise include survey use in market research, strategic thinking and planning, operational planning, results tracking, leadership and management development, team development and change management. Marie helps companies engage their customers and market more effectively to increase sales, profits and long-term competitive advantage.

Marie has worked with organizations from small to Fortune 500 companies, in both the public and private sectors, in a variety of industries. She also volunteers her professional services to specific non-profit organizations as a contribution to the community.

Marie's work on surveys, teams, leadership and other areas has been published by:

Competitive Edge Magazine

The CEO Refresher

Leader Values

Sabah Business (a business magazine published by one of the leading newspapers in Turkey)

RMIT University (Melbourne, Australia)

The Institute of Chartered Financial Analysts of India

Capital Magazine, with a circulation of 40,000 to business leaders in the Middle East, Africa, India, Pakistan and the CIS each month has published several articles on gathering market intelligence and building relationships with surveys by Marie.

Afterword and Gifts for You

How Can You Get More Help with Implementing the Survey Based Strategy in Your Company?

A. A complimentary, no obligation Executive Strategy Session is available with me about the use of a market survey strategy in your company. This is a strategy session. It is not about the nuts and bolts of doing market surveys. It is available for business owners and principals, V.P. or department head of Marketing or Customer Relations, CEO, COO, EVP and other persons who have decision making power about their company's marketing and/or customer relations strategies.

You can access the strategy session by going to www.mariejkane.com/yourstrategysession. This is a 45-minute consulting session wherein we will explore the fit of the market survey strategy for your company and consider your options. You will begin with my proprietary *Market IQ* assessment.

B. I have a gift for you at

www.MarketSurveyMastery.com/bookownersgift

On this page, you can download 2 of the 16 surveys from the *Quick Start Guide* in *Market Survey Mastery*. Here is a description of those two surveys.

1. Factors in Making a Buying Decision - This is a good survey to use when you are just entering a market and need to get familiar with what is important to your marketplace. Depending on your market, you might also add multiple-choice

questions on age, gender or other demographic data to this one. (Just a reminder: make sure you explore the core issues of your target market before embarking on this phase of your research.)

2.   Customer satisfaction survey for use with current customers that includes coverage on features, quality, price, value, ease of use and warranty.

C.   I strongly recommend that you take my FREE *Market IQ* assessment. You will find it extremely helpful in focusing what you need to address about your market knowledge and your processes for obtaining that knowledge. It is an excellent place to start. Here is the link to access it:

www.MarketSurveyMastery.com/BookOwnerMarketIQ.php

D.   If you have determined that the market survey-based strategy is a good fit for your company or organization and you want additional help on implementing the strategy, including specifics on creating, distributing and analyzing surveys as well as already prepared surveys, you have two options.

1.   My *Market Relationship Mastery Program* includes both group and individual company consulting as well as my comprehensive "how to" product (*Market Survey Mastery*). If you think you might be interested in this, then please see Item A above for a free strategy session. Together, we will explore the fit of the market survey strategy for your company and, if it is a good fit, what your options for implementation are.

2. My *Market Survey Mastery* product includes comprehensive "how to" information on all aspects of doing strategic surveys. For more information on this, please see www.MarketSurveyMastery.com. Readers of this book receive an additional 10% off whatever the current investment is by entering a coupon in the shopping cart, where indicated. Type this code word—bookowner, in the coupon field in the online shopping cart to get the discount. You must type it exactly as you see it here, all lower case and no spaces. Be sure to click "Apply," if indicated. The coupon will not activate if you do not.

E. If you choose to implement market surveys as described in this book and you document specific improvements in your business performance, I am interested in getting a testimonial from you for the book.   For qualifying businesses, I offer a free phone consultation, normally $1000.00, as my thank you gift to you. Proof of claims must be furnished to qualify for the free consultation. If you are interested in this, then I would love to hear from you at SurveyLadyMarie@gmail.com, Marie@MarketRelationshipMastery.com, or you can call me at 770-461-3820. I look forward to hearing from you!

Now a word about Jim and Carter

These two gentlemen are the colleagues who were so kind as to interview me for portions of this book. They are both consummate professionals whose services I have used for my own company. I have the utmost respect and confidence in each one of them.

Carter Harkins is the CEO of Harkins Creative, a digital creative agency that helps companies identify and tell their Brand's Story. In the role of Chief Storyteller, Carter spends time with business executives, asking key questions, discovering the places where a Brand's message is connecting with its market.   Perhaps more importantly, he intuitively listens for the cues that indicate where the message is falling short of delivering on the promise of the Brand, and together with his team of Brand Strategists, develops a comprehensive plan to begin telling the right story, at the right moment, to the right people.   Carter can be reached at carter@harkinscreative.com.

Jim Loesch helps local businesses obtain more traffic through using the latest Internet strategies to their advantage, showing them how to take over their local market.   He is dedicated to helping businesses achieve their goals and dreams.   As a lifelong student of marketing, Jim applies his vast knowledge in helping local businesses obtain and keep more customers/clients, ultimately, helping them to grow their bottom line.   Jim has a Win-Win-Win attitude.   Jim can be reached at jim@LocalIMPro.com.

Thank you for joining me on this journey about how you can use market surveys to grow your sales, profits and competitive advantage.   I wish you great success in implementing this strategy and substantially improving your company's performance.   Please let me hear from you about your experiences with this strategy as well as how I can help you more.   You can reach me at SurveyLadyMarie@gmail.com
Marie@MarketRelationshipMastery.com
770-461-3820

To Your Success!

Marie Kane
March 2010

www.ingramcontent.com/pod-product-compliance
Lightning Source LLC
Chambersburg PA
CBHW070403200326
41518CB00011B/2044